FANATICALLY RELENTLESS CUSTOMER SERVICE

The Insider's Guide:
How to
Rescue Your Customers
From a World of
Crappy Service

Calvin Stovall

TASORA BOOKS
Minneapolis • Minnesota

Copyright © 2008 by Calvin Stovall

Published by TASORA BOOKS
3501 Hwy 100 South, Suite 220
Minneapolis, MN 55416

All rights reserved. The text of this publication, or any part thereof, may not be reproduced in any manner whatsoever without written permission from the author, except by a reviewer, who may quote brief passages in critical articles or reviews.

Printed in the United States of America
Cover Design and Illustration by Jess Perna

Library of Congress Cataloging-in-Publication Data have been applied for.

ISBN 10: 1-934690-03-1
ISBN 13: 978-1-934690-03-1

For information about special discounts for bulk purchases, please contact Itasca Books.

Itasca Books
3501 Highway 100 South
Suite 220
Minneapolis, MN 55416, U.S.A.
www.itascabooks.com
952.345.4488

*This book is dedicated to my loving mother, friend and spiritual guide, Valerie Stovall.
I miss you very much.*

And most important, I would like to thank the Almighty God for giving me the strength and courage to step out on faith and do His work.

Contents

Preface		v
Shout-Outs		viii
Chapter 1	Boldly Take Your Customers Where No One Has Gone Before	1
Chapter 2	Customer Fanatics Drink the Water	18
Chapter 3	Successful Companies Value the Cracker Jack Principle	27
Chapter 4	Administer C.P.R. When Making Service Upgrades	37
Chapter 5	Are Your Customer Relationships Headed for Divorce?	49
Chapter 6	Don't Let Your Customer's Voice Fall on Deaf Ears	63
Chapter 7	We're Not in Kansas Anymore	73
Chapter 8	Jane, Stop This Crazy Thing!	82
Chapter 9	You're Fired! It's Not Just Donald's Tagline Anymore	96
Chapter 10	Are Disengaged Employees Sinking Your Business?	103
Chapter 11	Service Recovery Malfunction and the Baked Potato	116
Chapter 12	The Implode Effect and Its Impact on Your Bottom Line	128
Chapter 13	Show 'Em the Love!	135

Contents

Chapter 14	Is Great Service Burning a Hole in Your Pocket?	139
Chapter 15	A Fish Rots from the Head Down	147
Final Thoughts		156
Sources		159
About the Author		161

Preface

Can somebody please tell me what happened to customer service? Remember the good old days when you actually got a real person on the phone when you needed help? When waiters actually *waited* on you? When sales reps listened to you as opposed to shoving their products down your throat? When bank tellers didn't ignore you as they carried on with their paperwork? When hotel desk clerks made you feel like they were happy to have you stay with them? When companies fulfilled their brand promises made to their customers?

Peter Drucker said that the only reason for a company's existence is "to create and serve customers." What the heck is going on? Why is customer service today so crappy?

According to a 2007 poll conducted by America's Research Group, a consumer behavior research firm, one in four shoppers said they walked out of a store because of poor customer service. In the famous words of our timeless friend Forrest Gump, "Life is like a box of chocolates . . . you never know what you're gonna get." Sadly, the same applies to customer service in today's marketplace.

Having worked in the service industry for practically all of my life, I've come to one major realization when it comes to customer service – it isn't rocket science. When I was working for Hilton Hotels Corporation, Rick Schultz, a senior vice president with the company, used to always say to me, "Stovall, this business isn't difficult. People make it harder than it needs to be. Just take care of the customer." Since I've known Rick, he's always been a straight shooter. I have always liked that about him.

The underlying principles of delivering exceptional customer service are quite simple. We can tag it with many fancy titles, introduce complicated processes, and even integrate the best technology money can buy. But when you break down the recipe of what it takes to deliver quality customer service to its simplest form, it's not difficult to see why some companies are more successful at it than others. The successful ones understand, embrace, apply and deliver the basics of customer service on a consistent basis. They live and breathe by a simple business code: the CUSTOMER is KING (or QUEEN).

Being a professional speaker, I'm always looking for the newest and most innovative practices to keep my presentations as fresh as possible. I owe that to my customers. Yet, after reading so many books and articles on customer service, I have come to the realization that the secret to delivering fanatically relentless customer service (FRCS) simply lies in a "consistent execution of the basics."

This insider's guide was written for one purpose: to help companies take their customer service to the next level – without all the fancy language, high-powered lingo, jargon and difficult processes. At the conclusion of each chapter, I've listed several Fanatically Relentless Questions (FRQs) to help you think about (or rethink) how you're approaching your customer service initiatives from the company's, customer, team and leadership perspectives.

So there you have it . . . the reasons why I decided to write this guide. When I was a little boy, my momma used to always tell me, "Don't make a mountain out of a molehill." Simply translated, don't make things more difficult than they need to be. All this guide has for its readers is commonsense stuff everyone from the front line up to the C-suite can easily understand and apply on a day-to-day basis and truly become the customer service superhero in the eyes of their customers.

Enjoy!

*S*hout-*O*uts

To All My Fanatically Relentless Supporters . . .

My loving wife, Taisha Danielle. Thanks so much for your support and patience, and constant motivation ☺ to live out my purpose and finish this book. I love you, Babydoll!

My loving family, Pops (Calvin, Sr.), my younger brother Kevin . . . I love you, boy, and my baby sis' Starr, Grandma (Eleanor Burke) and a cast of beautiful aunts, uncles, cousins, nieces and nephews. Thanks for always being there for me.

Thanks to a host of friends, co-workers and colleagues at Hilton Hotels Corporation, Jim Holthouser and the entire Homewood Suites by Hilton brand team. Rick Schultz, Jim Hartigan, Lashell Vaughn, Susan Drake, Dusky Norsworthy and Linda Lobb. I appreciate all of your support in making this happen.

Lastly, to my two favorite ladies and mentors who helped me get to where I am today, Gloria Cooke and Karen Sock. Thanks for believing in me even at times when I didn't. The both of you will forever hold a special place in my heart.

FANATICALLY RELENTLESS CUSTOMER SERVICE IS:

ONE OF A KIND OVER-ENTHUSIASTIC, UNWAVERING, MOVE LIKE YOU MEAN IT CUSTOMER SERVICE

Chapter

1

BOLDLY TAKE YOUR CUSTOMERS WHERE NO ONE HAS GONE BEFORE

My wife, Taisha, and I relocated to Minneapolis in 2005 to launch our business venture. Despite the harsh winters, we love the Twin Cities. Besides, growing up in Chicago, I couldn't imagine winters being any worse. Even my southern belle, Taisha, loves it in Minneapolis. After living there for a few months, we began to explore the city for the hot spots, especially the good restaurants.

Both of us are huge breakfast fanatics. We love the stuff. To me, there's nothing better than a good conversation with someone you love while chomping down on some eggs, pancakes and hash browns and sipping on a hot cup of dark roast. You can't beat it. We like to eat at local restaurants for breakfast because they typically offer us a little more ambiance. While on our quest for the best breakfast eateries, every Minnesotan we asked offered us an enthusiastic, "You've gotta go to Al's Breakfast in Dinkytown. The food is absolutely great!" Hey, that's all my wife and I needed to hear. Now we're off to the races.

We get there and from the outside it looks like a typical restaurant front. But there's a line outside about 20 people deep. It looked like a line to get into a nightclub or something. I looked at my wife and excitedly said, "Baby, this place must be really, really good. Look at all these people in line." I'm salivating now. Ten minutes, 20 minutes, 30 minutes, 45 minutes, and we've only gotten up to the restaurant door. I'm still cool, though. We're getting there. After about an hour-and-15-minute wait, we finally make it inside the restaurant and I couldn't believe what was I was seeing.

The customer experience is becoming the new battleground for competitive advantage.

Al's Breakfast diner is all of ten feet wide! Built on top of an alleyway and once a storage area for plumbing parts used by the store next door, Al's is reportedly the narrowest restaurant in the city of Minneapolis, and possibly the narrowest full-service breakfast diner with counter-only seating in the world.

"Is this place for real?"

Once inside, to my left were several coat racks hanging on the wall and to my right, a long linoleum countertop that housed only 14 stools. We stood in line along the back wall of the restaurant with about three feet between us and the eating customers who were lucky enough to get there before us. The wall opposite the counter top was full of newspaper and magazine cutouts bearing awards and praises for the diner. About every 15 minutes or so, one or two guests would complete their meal, get up and squeeze by the folks in line, and the next up took a stool.

The servers took orders and yelled, "Two dark!" for two pieces of wheat toast, and faces old and new enjoyed the upbeat and friendly atmosphere. Frequent customers can purchase "meal books" that consist of 20 tickets and prepay for their food.

In operation since 1950, Al's has won the hearts of many Minnesotans and first-time visitors. The restaurant has served generations of students, along with notable writers, actors and political figures, all of whom consider the cramped diner to be an important icon of the state. A cast of regulars can be found there on any given day, sipping cups of coffee, making new friends, reconnecting with old ones and reliving old stories.

When you go to Al's, you don't simply have breakfast. This small place has something for everyone, except elbowroom. Anyone who steps foot into the ten-foot-wide, 14-stool-long breakfast-only joint located in the heart of Dinkytown will experience something that can't be duplicated anywhere. My wife and I enjoyed a good breakfast, good conversation and employees who entertained us as much as they cooked and served. The experience was fanatically relentless.

The customer experience is becoming the new battleground for competitive advantage. The successful companies of the future will be the ones who focus on creating memorable experiences for their customers as opposed to simply completing transactions. People don't talk about transactions, they talk about experiences.

IT'S ABOUT THE EXPERIENCE

On an almost daily basis, I've heard the phrase "customer experience" on the lips of my colleagues, consultants and marketers alike. *Customer experience* is now the hot buzz word. Could it be? No more lip service? Are companies finally beginning to look at the customer experience more closely? Are more organizations truly embracing customer-centricity (fancy word, huh)? Are they finally seeing the light and understanding how delivering a memorable customer experience can lead to competitive advantage? Whoa. Not so fast, cowboy.

According to an early 2007 report by the University of Michigan's American Customer Satisfaction Index

(ASCI), overall, consumers' perception of quality was virtually unchanged in the fourth quarter, while their perception of value rose 3.8 percent. David VanAmburg, managing director of the ASCI, stated, "The numbers do not necessarily indicate that shoppers are having a better experience, but it does suggest that they are finding better deals." He went on to say, "The quick and easy route to improve sales is to offer more promotions.

"Breaking from the pack requires you to lead customers to a place they didn't ask to go and didn't know existed."
Oren Harari, author of *Break from the Pack*

The slow and difficult strategy is to improve the shopping experience. Department stores appear to have settled on the quick and easy route." This is the perfect example of how not to create loyal, raving fans and advocates. I hope you agree, particularly in service industries, that simply competing on price and promotions is a short-term, quick-fix strategy and breeds brand promiscuity.

I'm drawn to companies that create memorable customer experiences on a consistent basis. I love Panera Bread. The employees are always friendly, they tantalize you with the desserts and cookies on display, your sandwiches and salads are made fresh, and the environment is always lively and upbeat. They offer free Wi-Fi, so I'm there quite often using the restaurant as my remote office. The shortbread cookies are great too!

Starbucks is another company that does a great job of creating an experience for its customers. When I want to get away from the office, I sip on a cup of dark roast while checking my e-mail at their coffee shops. When I travel, I rent my car from Enterprise and I stay at Hilton brands. I purchase my electronics from Best Buy, and my books, CDs and DVDs from Amazon.com. These are brands that I trust and they deliver time and time again.

Think about your own lives. Many of you probably fly Southwest Airlines, own an Apple computer, perhaps an iPod; some of you may even be HOGs (Harley-Davidson Owners Group) – people so passionate about their brand that they get tattooed with the Harley logo. You can't find a more passionate group of customers than that.

These companies know the secret recipe to creating and building a loyal fan base. Successful companies make a connection that transcends the basic functional value they provide to their customers. Customers perceive value based on the experiences they receive. Creating that emotional bond with your customers is the most effective way to take your company to the next level and build a more sustainable competitive advantage.

Successful companies make a connection that transcends the basic functional value they provide to their customers.

In a recent article entitled "Serenata Flowers Gets Personal," writer Chelsea Pritchard discusses how

Serenata Flowers, one of the largest independent online florists in the U.K., delivers not just flowers but also top-notch service. The company serves customers directly, instead of following a traditional network approach. This allows the company to own the entire customer experience. The company is dedicated to creating as dazzling a customer experience for those who send the flowers as for those who receive them.

"We have the basics down, like payment and delivery confirmation, but we've added more," says James Saunders, Serenata's head of e-business development. The company sends personalized e-mails to customers. It also reaches out to customers by sending text message reminders and offers directly to their cell phones and other mobile devices. The company keeps track of the special occasions for which each opt-in customer has ordered flowers, including holidays, anniversaries, birthdays and other personal special occasions. After every purchase, the company asks customers to fill out a survey via e-mail. If a customer gives Serenata less than a perfect 10 in overall satisfaction, the company will try to pinpoint and fix the source of dissatisfaction.

More than 80 percent of Serenata Flowers' customers say they will recommend the florist without hesitation. Moreover, the company has seen an impressive 20 percent month-over-month growth rate.

Boldly take your customers where no one has gone before!

You'll be surprised at how far it will take you.

MOMENTS OF IMPACT

What's the secret to delivering a memorable customer experience? Why are some companies like Zappos.com, Southwest Airlines, Starbucks Coffee, Nordstrom Department Stores and Amazon.com great at it and other companies are absolutely lousy? Simply, the aforementioned companies understand the importance of Moments of Impact.

Moments of Impact (MOIs) are those once-in-a-lifetime, precious opportunities to impact the customers' overall experience, and they include every interaction they will have with your company. MOIs will leave a positive or a negative impact on the customer. The secret to delivering a memorable customer experience is to ensure that each employee leaves a positive impression on the customer at every point of contact. The thing about MOIs is that every team member has to understand how important his or her role is to the entire customer experience. What many companies fail to understand is that every person who touches the customer – be it physical or virtual – is ultimately a part of the overall customer experience. Every MOI counts! Some more than others, but they ALL count. If one department or person delivers a negative MOI, everyone loses. Every employee needs to understand and take advantage of each MOI opportunity because when that happens, everybody wins – the customer, the company and the employee.

MICHAEL'S MOMENT OF IMPACT

I recall Elizabeth, a dear friend of mine, telling me about an experience she and her adorable four-year-old boy named Michael had while staying at an Embassy Suites hotel one weekend. I can't recall exactly which hotel it was, but it's a pretty cool story that stuck with me. Elizabeth said that she and Michael were standing in the hotel lobby early one Saturday morning enjoying the fish swimming in the pond. For those of you who have ever stayed in an Embassy Suites, you know how spectacular their lobby atriums can be, filled with greenery and sometimes a waterfall and pond.

Moments of Impact are those once-in-a-lifetime, precious opportunities to impact the customers' overall experience, and they include every interaction they will have with your company.

A maintenance person with the hotel walked up to them, holding a small bag in his hand. It's time to feed the fish. He introduces himself, and looks down at Michael and says, "What's your name?" Michael replies. The maintenance guy then asks, "Would you like to help me feed the fish this morning?" An excited Michael shouts, "Yes sir!" Michael grabs the bag of fish food and goes to town. He's throwing fish food all over the place – except the pond. The fish are splashing and Michael is having the time of his life. It doesn't stop there.

Later that afternoon, after shopping all day, Elizabeth and Michael got back to the room and the red message light was flashing on their phone. The desk clerk informed her that they were holding a package at the front desk. Elizabeth wondered what it possibly could be because she wasn't expecting anything. They both headed down to the front desk and the clerk handed Elizabeth an envelope with Michael's name on it. She peeped inside, smiled and handed it over to her anxiously waiting son. To both of their surprise, inside was a small bag of fish food and an official hotel name tag personalized with Michael's name and the position of "Master Fish Feeder." She said that Michael was so excited about getting the name tag that he refused to take it off during the remainder of their hotel stay. Elizabeth's face beamed with joy when she was telling me this story. Can you imagine how many friends, relatives and colleagues she's shared this wonderful story with? What kind of impact do you think that experience had on her and her son? What does it mean for a hotel brand like Embassy Suites? In my opinion, that experience is nothing short of what I like to call a true Moment of Impact.

THE COST OF A NEGATIVE MOI

A few years ago, Taisha and I took a trip to Atlantis in beautiful Nassau, Bahamas. The resort was absolutely breathtaking to say the least. On the day of our departure, we had a connecting flight that left from Nassau with a plane change in Cincinnati, then off to our final destination, Memphis, Tennessee. The first leg of our flight landed in Cincinnati about two hours behind schedule. No surprise there, right? So we had about 30 minutes before our next flight took off. We realized that we had to go to another terminal to catch our next flight. We jumped on an airport shuttle and he scooted us off. Now, we're frantically running through the airport like that old O.J. Simpson TV commercial, just not as gracefully. We finally arrive at the attendant's desk and we see about ten very upset travelers. You could tell by the looks on their faces that things weren't going too well.

Despite the madness, Taisha and I were still riding high from our trip. We'd just got back from the Bahamas, mon. We were so cool. What could possibly ruffle our feathers at this point? We walked up to the airline attendant and handed her our boarding passes, and the machine made a strange noise. Have you ever heard a noise and you know it's not going to be good news? We looked up at her and this young lady said, "Y'all can't get on this plane. They sent a smaller aircraft and y'all got bumped." If that wasn't enough, she said it with the most "I couldn't care less" attitude I have ever witnessed. She offered no apology. No empathy whatsoever.

Everyone's role is essential to the customer experience because when it's all said and done, when things go right or wrong, the customer is only going to remember one thing – one brand, one company, one entity.

I needed to let this young lady know who she was dealing with. I was a vice president with a Fortune 500 company. You'd better recognize. So I started ranting and raving. "Listen, young lady, I have an interview with the *Wall Street Journal* tomorrow afternoon, and you *need* to find a way for us to get back to Memphis, Tennessee." I truly wanted to impress my wife with my power. No such luck, though. Next thing I know, we were being handed one of those wonderful overnight kits with the bendable toothbrush and Elmer's glue toothpaste. I did end up getting a couple of flight vouchers when it was all over. But it was like pulling teeth. Look, I travel all the time and I'm a big boy. I know things happen that are out of people's control. But all I can vividly remember is that noncaring attitude of that attendant. Today, I go out of my way to avoid flying with that airline. I avoid it like the plague. I know what you're thinking: which airline am I talking about? Hint . . . Don't Ever Leave The Airport.

Everyone's role is essential to the customer experience because when it's all said and done, when things go right or wrong, the customer is only going to remember one thing – one brand, one company, one entity.

Every company, small and large, has the ability to create memorable experiences for its customers. Yes, it does require some additional effort to make it happen. Nevertheless, this is the only way to truly create raving fans and advocates for your company. You have all the tools at your disposal to take your business to new heights.

1. Make it happen at Moments of Impact. Part of the value in your service comes in the overall experience you create for your customers. Make sure everyone in the organization understands the experience you're trying to create in the hearts and minds of your customers. Each employee plays a critical role in making that experience come to life, especially those who have direct contact with the customer. Each person should clearly know how to execute that experience on a day-to-day basis. The customer experience is the true differentiator. A shopping experience is a shopping experience, unless it's a Nordstrom Department Store shopping experience.

I'm a huge Starbucks fan. I know that they've had their share of recent challenges, but I'm confident they'll get it together soon. Simply put, one of the biggest challenges they've faced is competition. We have so many coffee shop options to select from today. We've got

Dunn Bros, Caribou Coffee, even McDonald's and Dunkin' Donuts have upgraded their coffee offerings. Despite that, I will still go out of my way for a cup of Starbucks coffee. Not just because they make a great cup of joe. I really like to visit their coffee shops for the experience they consistently deliver. Their partners (they call their employees partners) are always friendly, the shops are always clean and the coffee is always hot and fresh . . . every single time I go. Everyone in the organization, from the CEO down to its partners at the coffee shops, understands the underlying fundamentals of FRCS: *If we consistently deliver on the Starbucks brand promise, we will win our customers' affection.*

2. Get the basics right every time. You can create an exceptional customer experience simply by focusing on the basics. It's not always about the WOW. Consistently delivering on the brand promise and ensuring nothing negative happens can take you very far in this marketplace. The customer WOW has its place, but just getting the basics right can be a giant leap forward for many companies. In my experience, I've seen so many hotel companies create all these fancy CRM (Customer Relationship Management) initiatives and programs to strengthen relationships and build loyalty with their customers, but you get up to the room and it's filthy. You've just created a negative Moment of Impact. Focus on getting the basics right every time and you can't lose.

3. Train employees to become experts. I can't stress enough the importance of making sure your employees are well trained and knowledgeable about the products and services your company provides. Your customers look to them to provide solutions and help them get answers as quickly as possible. Your employees should be viewed as resolution experts and trained as such. One of the quickest ways for your company to lose credibility and diminish trust is to have poorly trained employees handling your precious customers. Invest the money to get your employees up to speed immediately upon hiring them. Proper training not only reduces the level of frustration for the customer, but for the employee as well.

Customer expectations have risen fourfold. When problems do come up, customers want solutions, not excuses, like you get most of the time. No company can afford not to properly train its employees. The only way to ensure that your line-level employees are able to take care of customer issues is to make sure that they are properly prepared to do so. Meaning you have to make sure that you provide them with the proper tools to do it.

During my Hilton years, from time to time I'd hear managers talk about how expensive training was to their organization. Sadly, these manager types fail to see the bigger picture and focus too much on short-term results. Their complaint is simply, "Why spend more money on training, when they're just going to quit and go work for one of my competitors for an extra 50 cents an hour?" The bigger question you should ask yourself is, "What if I don't invest in training my staff and they *do* stick around?" Invest the dollars to train your team today or risk losing valued customers tomorrow because front-line employees aren't capable of effectively resolving customer problems.

CHAPTER 1 FRQs

1. How would you best categorize your company? As a T.O. (Transactional Organization) or an E.O. (Experiential Organization)?
2. Does your company invest the necessary time and money to ensure that your customer contact employees are properly trained?
3. Have you looked at all of your company's MOIs to ensure that the "basics" are being delivered on a consistent basis?

Chapter

2

Customer Fanatics Drink the Water

You can lead a horse to water, but you can't make it drink – a simple yet powerful statement. Never before has this principle been more applicable to today's service organizations. When it comes to delivering exceptional customer service, you've got to want to do it. You've got to drink the water and become fanatically relentless about your customer service delivery.

In the book *Satisfaction: How Every Great Company Listens to the Voice of the Customer,* authors Chris Denove and James D. Power IV of J.D. Power and Associates list two very simple truths when it comes to customer satisfaction:

- **No organization will improve customer satisfaction unless it truly wants to.**

- **No company will want to make the commitment to improve until it sees the link between customer satisfaction and the bottom line.**

Denove and Power show companies that improved customer satisfaction more than doubled their shareholder value. And those whose customer service ranking declined lost more than a fourth of their value.

On the surface, you would think that most service companies could easily make the connection between customer satisfaction and profitability. Yet, we all know that's not the case. Being the customer service fanatic I am, it's sometimes disheartening when I hear about an organization's supposedly "customer-centric philosophy" only to find out that it was just another clever marketing ploy. On the brighter side of the coin, though, when a company appears to be serious about customer service and is actually taking action to make it happen, I'm truly excited about it.

My momma used to always tell me, "Son, talk is cheap." If she told you that she was going to do something, you could rest assured it was going to happen. She backed up her words with action. I admired that about her because she was a lady of action. A person can talk about stuff all day long, but until they put action to it, its all just jibber-jabber. A lot of organizations today can talk a good game. But until they decide to put action (and money) behind their promises, absolutely nothing remarkable is going to happen. Companies have to put the necessary financial and people resources behind their customer service initiatives, or it's all just visions of grandeur. To truly become a customer-focused organization, everyone from the front-line staff to the CEO has to support the efforts. If all of the employees, shareholders and other constituents aren't in agreement and aligned with the company's vision to become a more customer-focused organization, then it's all just garbage.

Customer-centric organizations function with the customer always at the forefront of their operations (see diagram on next page). When new products and services are being considered, the customer has involvement in the development process. Departmental silos and barriers are eliminated. Sales and marketing people are on the same page and understand that without a collaborative team effort and understanding of key customer needs, everyone loses. Even human resources views things from the customer's perspective. They realize that if the company's internal customers aren't happily engaged, it can have a direct negative impact on the external customer experience.

THE CUSTOMER-CENTRIC ORGANIZATION

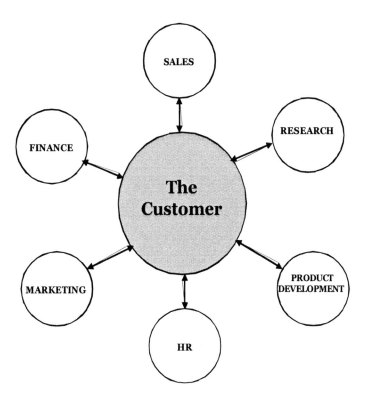

MANHATTAN BANK OF AMERICA

I recall reading an article in the *Wall Street Journal* about Bank of America and the company's planned onslaught to take over the Manhattan market. According to the article, New Yorkers could choose from among 95 financial institutions in that market. Talk about choices. However, Bank of America had managed to grow from just two years before, with no branches in Manhattan, to having 41. The bank's Manhattan deposits have grown to about $19 billion from less than $400,000 in 2001. Even more surprising is that almost half of the increase came in the 12 months ending June 2006.

They started drinking the water. The company became fanatically relentless about its customer service delivery. The bank implemented a "Bank of America Spirit" program. The program involves welcoming patrons and measuring "customer delight" by calling customers nightly who were in the branch that day for feedback. The bank has also adopted motivational techniques popularized by legendary companies like Disney.

Branch officers learn scripted sales pitches and carry laminated pocket cards listing key points of company philosophy. They start each morning with the "Daily Connect," a huddle in every branch to receive a sales motivation message. Branches are now designed with "onstage" areas for employees. Wall boards list staff birthdays and sales goals. The bank has converted tellers into salespeople, training them to meet monthly targets and selling financial products. Bank employees are not assigned offices, but instead are told to wear comfortable shoes because they're expected to spend time greeting customers. Way to drink the water, Bank of America!

SEA-MONKEYS LIVE AMONG US

When I was a handsome young tyke, among a ton of other interests, I was a big comic book fan. I loved Batman, Spidey, Ironman and the one and only Incredible Hulk. I was a comic fiend. But one of the most entertaining things for me was to flip through the last few pages of the comic books and look at all the strange items for sale – the X-ray glasses, onion chewing gum, magic rocks, squirting pens, silly putty and the infamous disappearing ink. I tricked my mother with that one a few times. Of course, I ordered all of them at least once during my childhood, and in most instances I was pretty happy with my purchase. However, I recall being absolutely fascinated by these intriguing little water creatures called The Amazing Sea-Monkeys. For those of you who have never heard of Sea-Monkeys, visit www.seamonkey.com.

I remember seeing them in my comic book for the first time. I was absolutely enchanted by these strange little water creatures sitting in their living room with their family. I had to have them! I placed my order and couldn't wait until they arrived. When my mother brought them to me from the mailbox, I read the directions very carefully to make sure that I didn't screw up. I then ripped open the little packet of Sea-Monkeys and poured them in the little aquarium filled with water and waited for something amazing to happen. But as some of you also found out, to my surprise, they weren't like anything I'd expected – not even close.

> *Unfortunately, our world is filled with Sea-Monkey-like companies. They come a dime a dozen.*

They just floated around like some kind of brine shrimp or something. I was absolutely devastated. What a letdown. As I got older, of course, I realized what geniuses these guys were; they were marketing aficionados! They created something that people purchased based on what they saw, but it truly wasn't what it appeared to be. Today, I use the term Sea-Monkeys for companies who are all talk and no action. I know it's a little strange. But what isn't strange, is that, unfortunately, our world is filled with Sea-Monkey-like companies. They come a dime a dozen.

Have you ever searched the Internet for a place to stay during your next trip and seen a collection of impressive hotel photos, but when you pulled up to the door the property looked like the housing projects? That's customer deception at its finest. Overpromising and underdelivering is one of the fastest ways to kill your brand reputation. Be honest and realistic when dealing with your customers.

Customers today have grown so tired of all the marketing hype. All the false promises made during television spots, on the Internet and in print ads. I'm not coming down on advertising. Hey, I'm a marketing guy. I love the stuff. But I *am* down on companies that make a brand promise and fail to follow through on that promise time and time again.

It doesn't matter if your company sells toys, shoes, laptops, cookies or spaceships. If you're dealing with customers on a day-to-day basis, whether you realize it or not, you're in the "people business." Successful companies understand that simple fact. Don't get me wrong, you do have to have a quality product to get into the customer's consideration set. But your company's continued success simply relies on its ability to emotionally connect and build meaningful relationships with its customers. Many companies are sadly disillusioned. Some think that it's all about "our product." Nothing could be farther from the truth. This kind of thinking will result in missed opportunities for long-term growth, profitability and success. Failing to understand that your business is all about the customers you serve every day will lead your organization down a reckless path of minimal differentiation and endless price wars in the marketplace.

CHAPTER 2 FRQs

1. Does your company recognize the connection between customer satisfaction and profitability?
2. Does your company just *talk* a good game about the importance of great customer service?
3. What challenges and roadblocks are keeping your company from delivering a seamless customer experience?
4. Do departmental silos and communication barriers exist within your company?
5. What are *you* doing *today* to improve your company's customer service delivery?

Chapter

3

SUCCESSFUL COMPANIES VALUE THE CRACKER JACK PRINCIPLE

Let's face it: products today have become so commoditized, consumers are finding it harder and harder to differentiate across product offerings – a coffee shop from a coffee shop, a hotel from a hotel, a restaurant from a restaurant, an airline from an airline, a car rental company from a car rental company. Without the surprise inside, they are all just boxes filled with a list of services, products and features. A box is a box. The real differentiation happens when employees create the magic inside the box. That's what truly creates delighted, satisfied and loyal customers.

In his new book, *Break from the Pack: How to Compete in a Copycat Economy*, author Oren Harari says, "Organizations today compete in an arena marketed by 'me-too' mimicry and lots of commoditized products and services. Helping organizations stand out and win in a Copycat Economy is the most strategic challenge leaders will face." Most business leaders agree that competing on product innovation and price is short-lived at best and does not translate into competitive advantage anymore.

The real differentiation happens when employees create the magic inside the box.

Harley-Davidson, Amazon.com, Nordstrom and Southwest Airlines haven't enjoyed continued success simply because of their prices or products. It's all about the experience they consistently create for their customers. These extraordinary companies understand the philosophy behind the "Cracker Jack Principle."

THE SURPRISE INSIDE THE BOX

"Buy me some peanuts and Cracker Jack, I don't care if I never get back." Words from the famous 1908 baseball anthem "Take Me Out to the Ball Game," by Jack

Norworth, are belted out by avid baseball fans everywhere. It's hard to believe that Cracker Jack has been around for more than 100 years. Introduced at the Chicago World's Fair of 1893, the caramel-coated popcorn and peanut concoction received its landmark name in 1896 when, according to legend, creator F.W. Rueckheim's brother Louis offered the confection to a salesman, who proclaimed, "That's crackerjack!" The brothers agreed, patented the name, and a brand was born.

Cracker Jack has earned a place in the hearts and stomachs of millions of Americans. In 2004, the New York Yankees baseball team replaced Cracker Jack with the similar Crunch 'n Munch at home games. The club soon switched back to Cracker Jack after a public outcry that was swift, immediate and fanatical.

How can one account for the lasting popularity of Cracker Jack? Is it the friendly face of Sailor Jack and his dog, Bingo, on the front of the box? Could it be somehow linked to the secret formula which magically keeps those candy-coated pieces of popcorn from sticking together? What is Cracker Jack's secret? I think it has to do with two little words: *surprise inside*. In fact, Cracker Jack is considered the largest purveyor of toys, having distributed an estimated 23 billion toys since 1912, when the company began putting them inside each box.

One of the main ingredients that has helped Cracker Jack make a lasting impact, not to mention one of the first things that kids (and some adults) still look for when popping open a box, is simply "the surprise inside the box." The surprises have come in every shape imaginable, but they've always been the same size since I opened my first box when I was a little boy: tiny. But boy oh boy, did that tiny surprise make a huge impression. Remember those great tattoos? When you think about it, did you ever purchase a box of Cracker Jack for anything other than the surprise inside? I doubt it.

SUPERQUINN – NOT JUST YOUR TYPICAL BOX

Even a box like a supermarket can differentiate when its strategy is purely focused on delivering a surprise at every turn. Feargal Quinn, Ireland's "pope of customer service," founded a chain of supermarkets called Superquinn. For the company's relatively small size, its brand, impact and ambition are remarkable. Customers enjoy a slew of surprises inside the box throughout their shopping experience. The bakeries guarantee customers never buy bread more than four hours old. Everything looks farm-stand fresh because all of Superquinn's fruits and vegetables are delivered twice daily. Each batch of mushrooms, lettuce and melons is marked with the time it was picked, a picture and a biography of its grower. The aisles have signs encouraging customers to report "goofs" such as overripe produce.

The stores also house a professionally staffed playhouse where parents can leave young children while they shop. Shoppers can grab an umbrella at the check-out counter so they can stay dry as they watch their groceries being transferred to the car by an enthusiastic employee. Superquinn operates on the "Cracker Jack Principle" and consistently delivers a surprise inside the box.

DEFINE THE FRCS EXPERIENCE

When I conduct my customer service workshops, I typically begin the session with two questions: "How many of you have taken a flight, stayed in a hotel, or had dinner at a restaurant in the last 60 to 90 days?" Pretty much all hands in the room quickly go up. Then, I drop the bomb, "Of those who raised their hands, how many of you had such a wonderful flight, hotel or dining experience that you couldn't wait to tell your relatives, co-workers, colleagues and friends about it?" In a room of 100 or so people, I may get one or two raised hands. More than often, no hands will go up. Now, that's pitiful, isn't it? But whose fault is it that these people consistently receive less-than-stellar service? Is it the manager's fault, the customer's fault, the CEO's fault or the employee's fault?

One of the major problems I've observed with many service businesses is that senior management will demand exceptional customer service delivery from their employees, when in fact most people have never even seen, let alone experienced, what exceptional customer service is.

The FRCS experience you're trying to create for your customers has to be clearly defined for your employees to effectively deliver it.

The $60,000 question is, "What does FRCS mean to your organization?" Stephen Covey, in his book *The 8th Habit*, described a poll of 23,000 employees drawn from a number of companies and industries. He reported that only 37 percent said "they have a clear understanding of what their organization is trying to achieve and why." To put it bluntly, the FRCS experience you're trying to create for your customers has to be clearly defined for your employees to effectively deliver it.

Not providing your employees with a clear path and what it takes to deliver quality service is the same as asking someone in an unfamiliar town to drive themselves to a particular location without a map or directions. It's just not gonna happen. The Ritz-Carlton hotel chain maintains it leadership position in service delivery because their *Ritz Carlton Service Values* are very specific about what they expect from their employees. In short, you're responsible for defining to your employees what that FRCS experience should look and feel like within your organization. If you don't take the time to properly define it – trust me – someone else will. Then what you'll end up with are mediocre results, at best.

Here are several fanatically relentless pointers on how can you truly create competitive advantage and apply "The Cracker Jack Principle" to your operation?

1. Be a great listener. Take some time to truly listen to your customers. Customer expectations are a moving target, so having a reliable feedback mechanism is important. At Superquinn, when it comes to getting a feel for the customer, nothing beats "jumping the counter." Managers are required to spend time "in the customer's shoes," shopping, asking questions, lodging complaints and waiting in line.

2. Deliver a consistent experience. Nothing will kill a brand's reputation faster than product or service inconsistency. Make sure that everyone in the organization, from the boardroom to the front lines, clearly understands the kind of experience the company is trying to create for its customers. When service expectations aren't met on a consistent basis, customer trust is diminished.

3. Dare to be different. Successful companies understand how important it is to be different when it comes to creating a memorable customer experience. Personalize the experience in a way that surprises your customers. Being unique and different is the only way you can truly break away from the pack and create advocates for your company. Customers are willing to pay a premium for an exceptional experience. Did you ever think you would stand in line to pay $4 for a cup of coffee before Starbucks came along?

4. Demonstrate your passion. People love to do business with companies that are passionate about what they do. We are all in the people business. Understand that to get this right, it has to be about more than just the transaction because customers don't talk about transactions, they talk about experiences. And whether you're on the front lines or back-of-house, every employee plays an important role in making that magical experience come to life inside the box.

Frito-Lay purchased the Cracker Jack brand from Borden, Inc., in 1997. Just as customers change, Sailor Jack and his trusty dog, Bingo, have had a few makeovers as well. Cracker Jack often comes in a bag, and the prizes have changed. As opposed to the trinkets of old, you're more likely to get paper prizes, displaying riddles and jokes. But as we know, nothing ever stays the same: consumer expectations and demands continue to change and evolve.

In order for organizations to remain competitive in the future, they will need to stay close to the customer and consistently create those magical moments at every turn. You can rest assured, doing that exceptionally well will never go out of style.

CHAPTER 3 FRQs

1. Does your company focus on creating a *surprise inside the box* for its customers?
2. How often does senior management spend time on the floor talking with customers?
3. Do your employees (management and front-line) demonstrate passion for what they do?
4. Does your company try to differentiate itself in creating a memorable customer experience?
5. Have you defined the FRCS experience for all of your employees, stakeholders and other constituents?

Chapter

4

ADMINISTER C.P.R. WHEN MAKING SERVICE UPGRADES

In order to remain competitive, smart service organizations should constantly evaluate the *hows* and *whys* of their customer service delivery. Out of that discovery, some companies decided to launch a new program to enhance their current service offerings in hopes that it will bring them that extra competitive edge. I applaud companies that go through this process. It is so vital to a company's long-term success to evaluate the services they provide and continually ask the hard question: "How can we do it better?"

A 2007 survey by the American Hotel & Lodging Association found that the hotel industry was planning on spending as much as $5 billion on property upgrades like comfy beds, upgraded showers, trendier bars, and those wonderful flat-screen televisions we've grown so fond of. According to an article in *USA Today* that same year, of 9,300 U.S. hotels in the survey, 69 percent had upgraded their bedding; 72 percent were offering voice mail; 82 percent were offering wireless Internet; and virtually all were wired to offer cable or satellite television.

Even some college libraries are being reinvented and moving away from those serene places you once remembered. The goal is to attract today's technology-savvy students back into the library with buildings that blur the lines between library, computer lab, shopping mall and living room. At Valparaiso University in Indiana, the Christopher Center has undergone a $33 million transformation. The main entrance of the library opens into a room with a Steinway grand piano, black leather couches, and cozy alcoves with fireplaces. Robotic arms retrieve books in about 15 seconds after a request is made online. According to the *Wall Street Journal* article, student traffic jumped 43 percent in the first year after the new library opened. Now *that's* innovation!

But all that glitters is not gold. Sometimes doing things differently can cause customers to rebel. Southwest Airlines, throughout its history, had a "no assigned seating policy." Customers chose where to sit as they boarded the plane, which resulted in an average turnaround time (the time between when a plane pulls up to the gate and when it pulls away for the next take-off) that was 40 percent faster than their competitors.

> *It's an irrefutable truth: innovation is the pathway to continued success and growth for any company.*

In June 2006, in an experiment, the airlines assigned seats for flights out of San Diego, which led to significant resistance from longtime customers. While the experiment was clearly implemented to improve the level of service provided, management had not anticipated the negative effect on the overall customer experience.

It's an irrefutable truth: innovation is the pathway to continued success and growth for any company. However, what are some of the things you should consider before pulling the trigger on a new customer service program?

When breathing new life into your customer service delivery, make sure that you administer **C**: Consistency; **P**: Preparation; and **R**: Relevance.

1. Consistency. Whatever program you decide to move forward with, make sure that it can (and will) be delivered on a consistent basis with every customer, every time. Nothing frustrates customers more than receiving a different level of service each time they visit or call a company. This is particularly important for franchise businesses and established brands. Consistency has tremendous power when it comes to building customer loyalty. People buy from brands because they know what to expect. McDonald's is the king of consistency. A Big Mac is a Big Mac; whether you're in California or Alaska, it's still going to taste like a Big Mac. Don't ever underestimate the power of consistency.

You'll never be remembered for delivering fanatically relentless customer service if it only happens every now and then.

Service and product inconsistencies across stores will destroy your brand reputation over time. Customer dissatisfaction is inevitable when companies overpromise and underdeliver. Spend the necessary time with the people who will be responsible for executing the program at customer contact. Make sure that everyone in the organization, from the boardroom to the front lines, clearly understands the kind of experience the company is trying to create for its customers. When service expectations aren't met on a consistent basis, customer trust is diminished. Many times, programs are created in *ivory towers* without proper consideration of how they might impact the overall experience and the employees who are responsible for creating the *magic* on the front lines. You'll never be remembered for delivering fanatically relentless customer service if it only happens every now and then.

2. Preparation. When I was a hotel front desk clerk, one of the most frustrating things for me was not being properly trained and having the necessary tools to effectively execute a new program. This is where a lot of companies drop the ball. Invest your dollars in the right areas when launching a new customer service program. Don't try to cut corners when it comes to properly training those responsible for execution. Great programs are all for nothing without proper execution. Management is critical in this process. Management is responsible for ensuring that front-line employees have the tools they need to administer these programs effectively. When a customer experiences a service breakdown at an MOI, all of the premarketing efforts you've invested to get that customer to test-drive your product or service fly out the window. Remember, first impressions are lasting impressions. Execution means everything.

3. Relevance. When considering a new service enhancement, ask yourself **W.I.I.F.T.C. – What's In It For The Customer?** Is the enhancement truly going to add value? Will it save the customer time, money, or enhance the overall experience? Does it create a point of differentiation? Or are you doing it because everyone else is doing it? Be clear on why you're adding a new program and clearly understand how it will impact your customer base. The life span of a new service enhancement is becoming shorter and shorter because of this monkey-see, monkey-do economy we live in today. When you introduce something new to the marketplace – unless it's truly revolutionary – your competition is sure to follow suit given enough time. So make sure that your service enhancements are relevant and meaningful to your customers.

Always administer C.P.R. when thinking about new customer service enhancements. However, let's not forget that the only way to truly build loyal customers is to consistently deliver experiences that create value beyond mere satisfaction. A hotel with comfy 800-thread-count bedding, a bank with enhanced technology, or a call center with the best customer response system available is all for nothing if the employees are rude, unknowledgeable and lack passion.

Calvin's food for thought:
Hold your breath, and invest your dollars where you will receive the greatest return on your money – in developing, motivating and retaining your best people because they're your greatest asset.

CALVIN'S THREE KILLER Cs

Don't allow your organization to fall prey to what I call **Calvin's Three Killer Cs.** These are the three Cs that will kill and have killed a company's or team's winning streak. Let's go over each of the three Cs and highlight how they can damage your business and how to stay away from them.

1. Cuttin' Corners. *Sacrificing brand longevity for short-term gains.* I'm a huge advocate for looking at ways to increase efficiency and make more money. But the danger is that sometimes those efficiencies can be achieved at a cost to the brand far greater than you anticipated. It was June 1993, and I'd just completed the MPS graduate program at Cornell University's School of Hotel Administration. It was time to get a real job. Promus Companies (now Hilton Hotels Corporation) selected me to participate in their President's Associate program. Of course, I was very excited. I completed nearly three months of training at a Charlotte, North Carolina, hotel and then I was shipped off to work as an assistant general manager at a 220-suite Embassy Suites hotel in Memphis, Tennessee. After I had worked at the property for about one year, the company was looking at how they could leverage some of the same efficiencies our limited-service sister brand, Hampton Inn, enjoyed.

They brought in a new general manager and the first phase of the test program began. This meant eliminating several key positions required to delivering a delightful guest experience. Needless to say, when these positions were dissolved much of the responsibility landed on the laps of the remaining employees, including myself.

Calvin's food for thought:
Make all the money you possibly can, but make sure it's not at the sacrifice of delivering a consistent, high-quality product and service. Nothing will kill a brand faster than inconsistencies in either one of these areas.

Guess what? After a few months within the program, we saw our operating margins ticking upwards – as much as 10 to 12 points above the brand average. However, on the flip side of that coin, our customer service scores, productivity and morale were spiraling downward. This short-term strategy to improving financial performance negatively impacted the team and ultimately the Embassy Suites brand experience. Needless to say, this project was unsuccessful. All of the eliminated positions were eventually replaced – a valuable lesson learned.

2. Constriction. *Choking out room for creativity and innovation.* To get something you've never had, you have to do some things you've never done. Things never stay the same. Customer needs and expectations are constantly evolving. What worked in the past may not necessarily work today. Moving from good to great can only happen if you're willing to rewire the way you see things and trying some new ideas. Be creative and allow others on your team to be creative. Creativity is all around you. It's great to look to your external customers to solicit feedback and ideas. However, sometimes your best ideas will come from the people on the front lines. These are the people closest to your customers on a day-to-day basis. Invite them to participate in brainstorming sessions, and allow them to help you improve the level of service you provide for your customers. Your employees want to be solicited for their ideas and feedback. This collaborative approach not only will gain you some wonderful ideas but also will make your employees feel like they're a part of something greater. Moreover, you'll have their immediate buy-in because they helped create the program – a win-win for everyone involved. More than anything, people just want to feel like they belong and know that they play a vital role in the organization's success.

An essential element to ongoing business success and growth is keeping an open mind to trying some new ideas.

When a food manufacturer was trying to find out how to improve the changeover time of one of their assembly lines, it brought in an Indy race pit crew to demonstrate how to do it. Who has better mastered the talent of "working against time" than a group of people who can instantly change several tires in a highly coordinated team effort that lasts only a few seconds? It was an offbeat solution, but it certainly did the trick. Keep an eye out for the quirky, innovative and unusual things occurring within and outside of your industry.

3. Complacency. *Self-satisfaction without regard to competition.* As you know, complacency and reluctance to change have taken many companies under. You must constantly strive to achieve excellence, and look for new ways to take your performance to the next level. Staying stagnant is not an option. Don't ever get too comfortable. Even as you read this book, your competitors are designing strategies to lure your customers away from you.

NO RISK, NO REWARD

Of the three Killer Cs, I think constriction and complacency are the most dangerous. Why? They both deal with change in some form or another. We know what change does to some people, don't we? Change can sometimes cause a rebellion, especially when things have always been done "this way." Change can make some individuals' heads spin like Linda Blair's. But constant evaluation and analysis is the only way you're going to take your business to the next level. An essential element to ongoing business success and growth is keeping an open mind to trying some new ideas.

Encouraging risk taking within your organization is one effective method of ending constriction and complacency. Don't be afraid to try some off-the-wall ideas sometimes. You may try some things and they simply may not work out. That's okay. Not all that Starbucks touches turns to gold either. In 1999, they rolled out a coffee magazine called *Joe*; it lasted all of three issues. And a carbonated coffee beverage developed with PepsiCo never even hit the market. Don't let your fear of making a mistake get in your way. I read a wonderful quote in a book: *the person who doesn't make mistakes is unlikely to make anything*. Don't create an environment that punishes people for making mistakes because it stifles creativity. Failures and challenges are prerequisites of success.

CHAPTER 4 FRQs

1. When your company makes product or service upgrades or enhancements, are the necessary steps taken to ensure that they can (and will be) delivered on a consistent basis?
2. Would you consider your company to be cutting-edge or complacent?
3. Does your company involve its employees in the creative process, including brainstorming sessions, when developing new product and service enhancements?
4. Does your company spend enough time looking at how to do things better and improve service delivery?
5. When did your company last introduce a new program to improve customer service delivery?

Chapter

5

ARE YOUR CUSTOMER RELATIONSHIPS HEADED FOR DIVORCE?

Why don't you listen to me?
Why is it so difficult for you to say I'm sorry?
Why don't you talk to me?
Why do you treat me this way?
Why can't you take responsibility for your mistakes?
Why don't you care?
Do you really want this relationship to end?
How could you betray me?

Are these comments from a marriage counseling session with Dr. Phil? Not quite. These are comments from your customers who are not feeling the love. How much are your customers worth to you? Many companies today don't realize the critical mistakes they make that push their customers away. Customers vote with their feet, and they make the decision to stay or leave a relationship based on their perception of how much they're valued and how well they're treated. Customers simply expect more than just a good product or a low price. They expect to be treated well and will settle for nothing less.

A strong customer relationship is critical to a company's success. Why? We know competing on price is a short-term approach and leads to diminishing profit margins. And while having a somewhat differentiated offering is essential for getting into the game, you are still vulnerable to the competition coming out with a similar or even better offering. Not to mention that customers have so many options to select from and can take their business to a competitor in a heartbeat if they feel unappreciated or you mistreat them just once.

If your customers aren't feeling the love, they feel no loyalty or obligation to hold on to the relationship.

I recall reading in an article that an average business loses 15 percent of its clients on an annual basis. We can make some basic assumptions why this happens. But the real truth is that many customers just stop coming because the company hasn't established a relationship with them. If your customers aren't feeling the love, they feel no loyalty or obligation to hold on to the relationship. Companies that keep their customers delighted tend to hold on to them. They have strong relationships with their customers and are also better able to bounce back when things do go wrong.

I'm sure you've heard the horror story. In mid-February 2007, the once "customer service darling" of the airline industry got stuck on the runway. JetBlue Airlines upset a lot of its customers. One thousand canceled flights over the course of a few days. Hundreds of passengers sitting on a plane for a full ten hours! Whew! Bring out the Arrid Extra Dry. Not soon thereafter, JetBlue published its "Customer Bill of Rights," promising customers differing voucher amounts for future flight delays and cancellations. The word is still out on whether JetBlue will be able to fully recover from this catastrophe. I hope so because I've always admired them for their commitment to delivering exceptional customer service.

A DINNER EXPERIENCE SERVED UP COLD

My wife and I love Benihana. Benihana is the name of a chain of Japanese restaurants known for its food as well as the experience. The food is prepared in front of the customers on a large hibachi. In mid-January 2008, my wife and I were invited to attend a birthday celebration, along with 11 other friends at Benihana Restaurant in

Maple Grove, Minnesota. We even brought our then six-month-old son, Caden Daniel, along for the party. We typically have dinner at another location closer to our home, but if you've been to one Benihana, you've been to them all. Well that's what I thought until that bone-chilling Saturday evening. The temperature outside that night was -2 degrees. Yes, -2 degrees! Now *that's* cold!

But so what? The party's on tonight!

When we arrived at the restaurant for our eight o'clock reservation, the hostess said, "We don't have any heat in the restaurant." I know, we should have turned around and left, but there were 13 of us and a baby. Where were we going to go and get seated for 13 1/4 folks at 8 o'clock on a Saturday evening? And besides, it was too cold to go back outside anyway. So we decided to stay.

Fact: *Forty-four percent of diners say they strongly agree that enjoying a dinner away from home "is as much about the experience as about the food."*
Restaurants & Institutions' 2008 New American Diner Study

So there we were, sitting around this huge hibachi with our coats and hats on like the rest of the restaurant patrons. My son was comfortably wrapped up like a burrito. I have to admit, the whole incident was kind of funny. Despite the humor, what I found most disturbing is that the restaurant manager never came over to our table to apologize. Mistake #1. As a matter of fact, he never even walked by to see how things were going. The only saving grace was the chef we had. He was great. During our conversation, the chef informed us that the heat had been out for a whole week. Our jaws dropped. You mean that you guys have been working in this cold restaurant for an entire week?

They did bring over some space heaters to try to make us feel more comfortable, but they just weren't making things any better. Following dinner, one of the waiters walked over to our table and said, "The person celebrating a birthday tonight gets a complimentary scoop of strawberry ice cream." Of course, the birthday girl quickly raised her hand. Yeah, I know what you're thinking? Who would want ice cream while sitting in an igloo? Hey, no one turns down ice cream! Being a frequent Benihana customer, my wife said to the waiter, "We always eat at the other location, and a scoop of ice cream is included in the dinner price." The young lady replied, "Well we don't do that here. If you want a scoop of ice cream, it's three dollars." Mistake #2. Mind you, we've been sitting here in the cold with our coats and hats on for the entire dinner. She should have given us a gallon of ice cream with no questions asked. I reluctantly agreed to pay for the ice cream, but I knew that this wasn't over by any means.

The total bill was a little more than $700. We said our good-byes and left the restaurant without even an apology. On the way home, I can tell that the whole experience was still bothering Taisha. She didn't say anything for the first five minutes or so. Then she couldn't hold it any longer. "Can you believe that they wouldn't give me a scoop of ice cream? That's just not right! As soon as I get the opportunity, I'm calling their corporate office and telling them what happened there tonight."

Remember, folks, strong customer relationships are built over time. It takes real commitment.

But to her surprise, she couldn't speak to anyone at the corporate office about her cold experience. Why? Because when she went to their website to get the phone number, there's no number listed to contact them. Mistake #3. They have an employee line. But if you're a customer, you're out of luck, Charlie. All you can do is fill out a comment form, which probably gets sent into oblivion somewhere. What a slice to the customer. Our relationship is in jeopardy. We're thinking about filing our divorce papers from Benihana.

But hold on! Could it be?

About two weeks after my wife sent in her e-mail, we received the following letter from Benihana in the mail:

Dear Mr. Stovall,

Thank you for your email regarding your dining experience at Benihana Maple Grove on January 19th.

The management and our construction department have been working on the heating issue in the restaurant with local companies. We apologize that we were not able to provide you with an enjoyable and comfortable family dining experience with your child.

It is very important to us to receive feedback from customers like you as a tool to improve on our quality of service and food. I really appreciate that you pointed out the issues. As a token of our apology and appreciation, I enclosed a dinner certificate which can be redeemed at any of our 60 direct units so that we can make your next visit to Benihana a positive experience.

We truly value your patronage and look forward to serving you again soon.

Sincerely Yours,

Steve Takenaka
Benihana, Inc.
TLC of Customer Relations Manager

Yes! Benihana *does* care about our relationship. Now that's how you slice up some reconciliation, guys. Thanks for getting our relationship back on track.

Even the strongest of relationships get tested from time to time. What steps can you take to ensure that your customer relationships stay intact? Just think about what it takes to have a successful marriage or any other long-term relationship.

1. Stay in the circle of trust. I love the movie *Meet the Parents,* starring Ben Stiller and Robert DiNiro. I think it clearly shows the importance of relationships (although a little dysfunctional), and it does demonstrate how a certain level of "uncertainty" exists until real trust can be established. The "circle of trust" is very real, especially when it comes to working in the people business. When a relationship is established, it becomes strengthened when the business creates a level of trust by consistently delivering on the customer's expectations over time. Not one time, not two times, not even three times, but every time. And the cool thing that is after trust has been established, if the company does drop the ball on occasion, guess what? The customer will love you enough by then to give you another opportunity. However, during the early stages of the relationship, the customer's tolerance level for customer service mishaps is very low. I've seen many customers switch to competitor because they were constantly let down. Until trust can be built and established in the relationship, there is no room for error. You have to get it right, every time. No excuses.

Nothing will make a company lose credibility and diminish customer trust faster than making a promise and not following through.

If a customer trusts your company, then you can be depended on to do what you say you will. There is a growing case of corporate amnesia in the world today that drives people crazy. A customer calls in an issue with his bank account and is promised it will be resolved and nothing happens. A customer returns a faulty product and is promised a replacement will be sent to her home and it never arrives. A customer makes a hotel reservation and is promised a room with a view and she gets a view of the back alley. Nothing will make a company lose credibility and diminish customer trust faster than making a promise and not following through.

2. Swallow your pride. Customer service issues are inevitably going to occur. If something goes wrong, don't make any excuses. Own up to it. Then do whatever it takes to get the relationship back on track. In JetBlue's situation, then CEO David Neeleman took the pilot's seat and reacted quickly with a sincere apology for the mishap. During an interview on NBC's *Today Show*, Neeleman said, "We're going to be held accountable."

When you take full responsibility to correct your mistake, a potentially damaging situation becomes an opportunity to win the customer's loyalty. There's nothing more frustrating to customers than a company that does something wrong and won't admit it. Customers will forgive incompetence, but not bad character.

3. Show some empathy. The best way to understand what your customers are thinking and feeling is by putting yourself in their shoes. Customer-focused companies put the customer's perspective before their own by thinking like their customers. According to the book *Exceeding Customer Expectations*, at Enterprise Rent-A-Car, workers at all levels are encouraged to constantly look around the office, hear how many times the phone rings before being picked up, look at the expressions on the faces of customers to see whether they are smiling or showing signs of frustration. It really comes down to the golden rule of treating customers the way you'd want to be treated yourself.

I learned this skill during my hotel days. I had to work some late nights when the hotel was oversold and we'd have to "walk" (not literally, it's hotel jargon) the guest to another area hotel, at our expense, of course. Let me make something perfectly clear: when it's 11:30 p.m. and a tired business traveler is told, "I'm sorry, Mr. Smith, but there's no room at the inn," it doesn't matter if you send them to Trump Towers for the night, it doesn't make a bit of difference. I truly felt empathy for the people who found themselves in this circumstance. Although I couldn't do much about it, I tried to make the experience as pleasant as possible for the customer. Now being in the professional speaking business, I've had a couple of "walk" experiences happen to me. Life is funny that way.

> *Customer-focused companies put the customer's perspective before their own by thinking like their customers.*

4. Keep it simple. Don't make it difficult for your customers to communicate with you. If you ask most customers, they'd say that the obstacle course at most companies for figuring out who to talk to and how and when to get service is overcomplicated, conflicting and just plain confusing. Too often, businesses require the complaining customer to jump through hoops or go through a great deal of effort to have any concerns properly heard. Some companies require customers to spend time writing a letter or posting a complaint with little or no opportunity to discuss the problem with an experienced person. Customers want someone who will take responsibility for the issue and direct the entire process through resolution. Always be open to discussing problems with your customers.

Remember, folks, strong customer relationships are built over time. It takes real commitment. Take a long-term view of things, not dwelling on this month's sales but understanding how loyal customers represent a stream of earnings over time. Keep in mind, customers will only do business in the future with companies that treat them well today. When you show your customers the love, not even the craftiest of your competitors can lure them away.

As my wife so kindly reminds me, "You've got to keep doing the same things you did to get me, in order to keep me."

SATISFACTION IS NOT ENOUGH

We all know that one of the key components in sustaining a successful business is keeping your customers satisfied. But is customer satisfaction enough? Absolutely not. I'm sure some of you know men and women alike who say that they are satisfied with their relationships, but aren't necessarily loyal to them. Am I right? The same holds true in the world of business. Customer satisfaction does not equate with customer loyalty. You can have a lot of satisfied customers, but what you want to have is loyal customers.

Loyal advocates can't live without you because your company is the only one that treats them that "special" way. When that happens, you know that you have a loyal relationship. Loyal customers will not only buy from you time and time again, they will also be your mouthpiece in the marketplace – your brand evangelists.

Customer satisfaction does not equate with customer loyalty.

Loyal customers are people of action and they will tell all of their friends, relatives, co-workers and colleagues about your company. The secret to moving beyond mere satisfaction to loyalty lies in cultivating a meaningful relationship with your customers and listening and responding to their needs – not once, not twice, but every time. And that's what great relationships are made of. Simply put, customer loyalty leads to competitive advantage.

CHAPTER 5 FRQs

1. Does your company value its customer relationships?
2. Does your company focus on building trust with its customers?
3. Does your company spend time strengthening and fostering its customer relationships?
4. Do your customer contact employees show empathy for customers when things go wrong?
5. How would you best describe most of your customers – just satisfied or loyal?
6. How easy is it for your customers to communicate with your company?

Chapter

6

DON'T LET YOUR CUSTOMER'S VOICE FALL ON DEAF EARS

D o y o u ever wonder what happens to all that customer feedback you provide to restaurants, car service centers, supermarkets, hotels, airlines and car rental companies? If you're like me, you can't help but think all that valuable information you offered is sitting in a database somewhere, rotting away like a carcass in the desert. Why? Because it seems like the customer experience at most service companies never changes. Even after you've expressed your dissatisfaction online, on paper and on the phone, it's the same rude desk clerk, the same grueling loan process, the same tech support, the same phone prompts, the same long wait for your meal – the list goes on and on.

According to a Customer Champions in European Companies study, 95 percent of companies collect customer feedback; 50 percent alert staff to the findings; 30 percent make decisions using this insight; 10 percent deploy and improve; and lastly, only 5 percent inform customers of the change.

> *Companies that truly listen to the customer will ultimately lead the pack when it comes to customer satisfaction.*

I think one of the most important factors to delivering FRCS is making sure that you spend time discovering, listening, learning and finding out customer needs on a regular basis. Why? Customer needs and expectations change all the time. Companies that truly listen to the customer will ultimately lead the pack when it comes to customer satisfaction. I know a lot of companies talk about how much they "listen to their customers." But the real question is, what do they actually do with the information? Only a chosen few actually listen to their customers *and* take action on their recommendations.

Use the Voice of the Customer (VOC) to break away from the pack and outsmart your competition. There's significant value in the learning relationship you can build with your customers over time. When was the last time you spent some time listening to your customers?

Did you find out something about your customers that your competitors don't know? How can you use VOC to enhance value, increase satisfaction and strengthen loyalty? Also, be careful not to get too caught up in numerical scores. The changes you make should be based not only on scores but also on the insight you gain from customers' comments. Scores are nice, but you want your VOC program to open your eyes to the kind of insight that will help you deliver "surprises" and truly differentiate you from your competitors.

Determining your customers' needs and expectations is no simple task, but VOC can help take some of the guessing game out of the equation. This isn't about which VOC approach is best or most effective. It's about really acting on the insights you gather to improve the experience for your customers. It doesn't matter if you use some VOC software for compiling customer feedback, a paper-based questionnaire or an online survey. What's most critical is that you actually do something.

DON'T DRINK TOO MUCH OF YOUR OWN KOOL-AID

In my opinion, we live in a business world that relies too heavily on its own intelligence. Many companies operate in a vacuum. They think they've got all the answers. They always know what customers want and what they need. If you ask me, many companies drink way too much of their own Kool-Aid. A lot of organizations talk a good game about listening to customers. Companies need to listen to their customers to show how much their opinions and feedback are valued. Customer expectations are a moving target, so having a reliable feedback mechanism is important.

To be effective, companies must trust the voice of their customers and act on what they are trying to tell them. If you want to improve your customer relationships you need to see things from your customer's perspective. Far too often, companies only listen to their own voices as opposed to the voice of the customer. Some of the biggest marketing blunders in history are the result of companies thinking they know what's right for their customers, even when their customers are doing everything possible to tell them to go in another direction. Ford Motor Company's ill-fated Edsel is one of the more notorious examples.

Today, our world has become more and more sophisticated about how to better connect with customers. But the simplest approach is sometimes the most effective, and that's listening. Genuine listening ability is one of the few true forms of competitive advantage. The best listener wins the game!

PUTTING VOC INTO ACTION

General Electric Co. uses a tool called "Net Promoter" for tracking customer satisfaction. According to a *Wall Street Journal* article, the tool allows GE to track and quickly address customer concerns. GE asks customers to rate on a scale of zero to 10 "how likely they would be to recommend the company to a friend." Survey respondents who rate GE a 9 or 10 are categorized as *promoters;* those who gave GE a 7 or 8 are rated as *passives;* and those who rate GE at 6 or lower are dubbed *detractors.*

GE Capital Solutions has been surveying about 1,000 of its 1 million clients each month since early 2006. In September 2004, business-loan processing took six months. Armed with scores and customer comments, processing steps were reduced by one-third, and now similar business loans are processed in five days or less, on average.

When Pulte Homes, Inc., wasn't satisfied with the scores it was getting from customers in 2001, it created a customer relations department of 1,200 people and established a program to ensure that it paid closer attention to its customers' desires throughout the sales and building process. Pulte is now tracking its customers over a long period of time.

First Pulte surveys its buyers immediately after purchase to find out how they feel about their home.

Then the company circles back several years later to make sure buyers are still pleased. This VOC approach has helped the company's repeat and referral business grow from 20 percent in 2001 to 45 percent of the company's revenue. In recent years, Pulte has won more J.D. Power & Associates awards than any other new home builder.

> *"Our goal is to make sure we are listening to what customers are telling us. We are looking at their eating habits, what the trends are, their lifestyles."*
> Don Thompson, president of McDonald's USA

You too can make VOC work for your organization, but it takes more than just gathering information. For VOC to make a real impact, it takes an organizational commitment to leveraging the feedback to improve the experience for your customers.

1. Be a brand of action. Gathering feedback simply isn't enough. Companies must act on the insight they receive. Companies are raving about the Voice of the Customer and how important customer feedback is to delivering a great customer experience. No question about it, VOC can be very profitable when applied properly. It can lead to the creation of a superior product or service, identify and prioritize customer needs, improve internal processes, enhance service delivery, strengthen customer relationships and even foster customer loyalty.

If an entity is going to take up customers' valuable time finding out how they feel about their service experience, the company owes those customers the common courtesy of at least reviewing the feedback and then making feasible changes to enhance the customer experience. Regardless of the method a company uses to track customer satisfaction, it's all fruitless unless some reasonable changes in how it conducts business are made based on that feedback.

2. Foster a listening culture. Develop a customer listening system that includes regular customer panels, an 800 number, customer-comment cards and/or formal market research. If cost is a concern (and when isn't it?), simply make quarterly calls to your top customers to get their feedback on your product or service.

Create and foster a work environment where your employees monitor the voice of the customer in their interactions with them. Employee listening should be validated and feedback encouraged even if it's negative. Even the most dissatisfied customer can be a valued source of learning. Inform and educate everyone within the organization on the business advantages of customer feedback. Moreover, the value of customer feedback increases exponentially when it's shared. Eliminate the silos and share relevant VOC research findings throughout the organization. Don't forget to get everyone involved in your VOC efforts, including your customers, partners and other business constituents.

3. Manage the store – not the score. In the book *Satisfaction*, Chris Denove and James D. Power IV discuss how employees can sometimes become too concerned with the customer satisfaction score and lose focus on the real goal of building customer advocates. When employees place too much emphasis on the scores, they are tempted to pester customers to answer surveys in a favorable way. This can result in just the opposite of what you were after when you began surveying your customers by frustrating the very people you were trying to satisfy. Lastly, be careful how you provide employee incentives for customer satisfaction and take precautions to avoid implementing programs that are easy to manipulate.

4. Leverage the power of Web 2.0. I could write an entire book on all the social media opportunities available in the marketplace today. Social media and networks are seen as the future of marketing and customer engagement. Sadly, a lot of companies are just jumping on the bandwagon because it seems like the cool thing to do and are seeing little ROI for their efforts. Done right, with a well-thought-out strategy, these online communication vehicles can indeed improve and strengthen customer relationships. How can you utilize this feedback to enhance customer engagement? What are they saying about your company in the marketplace? How can this feedback be used to help you better target your customers? Encourage your customers to express themselves in social networks, blogs, wikis, and the like, and then learn from their behavior and take action.

CHAPTER 6 FRQs

1. Does your company have a VOC strategy in place?
2. Does your company actively listen to and respond to your customers' feedback in a timely manner?
3. What does your company do, if anything, with the feedback it collects from its customers?
4. What kind of listening posts does your company have in place *now*?
5. Is your entire organization involved in the customer feedback process?
6. Do you share satisfaction scores with everyone in the organization, especially customer contact employees?
7. Does your company have a strategy in place to leverage social media networks (if applicable)?

Chapter

7

WE'RE NOT IN KANSAS ANYMORE

This one-liner from the classic movie *The Wizard of Oz* couldn't be more relevant to what we're experiencing in today's marketplace. In a recent *Wall Street Journal*, I ran across a "Pepper . . . and Salt" cartoon. The cartoon shows Santa pulling a single letter from his mailbox. His elf looks at him and says, "Only one letter. I told you we should switch to email or texting." My, my, my . . . times have really changed.

"Calvin, can you talk about the challenges of Generation Y employees and their impact on customer service?" This is a common question during my customer service workshops. When someone asks that question, I typically hear sighs move across the room and watch as people roll their eyes, frown or shake their heads. But during a recent workshop, a young lady in her early 20s asked me a question that intrigued me: "Calvin, do you think organizations are ready to change the way they do business to service the younger generations, specifically the Gen Xers and Ys?" Knowing how challenging it can be for people, let alone organizations, to change, her timely question prompted me to write this chapter.

Companies are now beginning to wake up to the potential of these future customers because these are the folks who will dominate the marketplace for the next 70 years or so. As the baby boomers begin to retire, organizations must come to the realization that they have no choice but to adapt and accommodate Gen Xers and Ys. Understanding what it takes to attract and keep them happy is the only sure-fire way to guarantee your organization's continued growth and relevance in the marketplace.

SAY HELLO TO YOUR FUTURE CUSTOMERS

Meet Generations X and Y – also known as "Generation Next." They're ambitious, they're talented, they're high maintenance, they're outspoken, they're tech savvy, they're demanding, and they question everything. They have completely different values, expectations, needs and desires than the baby boomer generation before them. When it comes to loyalty, the companies they work for fall last on their list – behind their families, their friends, their communities, their co-workers and, of course, themselves. They are some of your hottest target customers, and there are plenty of them. But what makes them so different?

Gen X and Y consumers walk in with more information in their heads and at their fingertips than the generations before them. They're so connected that it's not unusual for them to know what every major company in a given field is offering. They are very accustomed to walking away from something (or someone) that fails to meet their expectations. They know they have an abundance of choices and have no problem taking their business to a competitor if a company fails to deliver on their promise. They aren't impressed by mission statements and clever marketing ploys and antics. What they are looking for in a company are attributes that indicate shared values and authenticity. The best way to attract the attention of the newest generations of buyers is be authentic and "keep it real."

Last year, Ritz-Carlton dropped 20 strict rules governing employee behavior in favor of commonsense principles that allow employees to respond more naturally to guests. Additionally, the upscale lodging chain launched a new campaign as part of a larger effort to loosen its stiff image and broaden its appeal among younger consumers. To attract consumers to its Web site, the chain created several short films with online trailers and posted them on Yahoo, MSN and YouTube.

Gen X and Y consumers walk in with more information in their heads and at their fingertips than the generations before them.

Environmental, health, social and ethical issues are a hot button with younger consumers. The newer generations are significantly more likely than previous generations to consider companies' practices when making buying decisions. Companies should do a better job publicizing their corporate social responsibility efforts. Spelling out your organization's stand on social, environmental and other issues is an effective way to attract these younger customers.

Chipotle Mexican Grill's chairman and chief executive Steve Ells is pushing for other fast-food chains to pressure suppliers to raise animals more naturally and humanely and produce ingredients in a way that is more environmentally sustainable – an approach Mr. Ells calls "food with integrity."

Is your organization prepared to meet the unique needs and expectations of Generations X and Y? To help you get the ball rolling, I'd like to offer you the **Three Cs of Generation Next** – **C**onnectivity, **C**ustomization and **C**ommunity – to better position your company to meet the needs of these younger consumer groups.

1. Connectivity. They have never known a world without remote controls, CDs, cable television, and the PC. They are the most technologically savvy, educated and wired people to walk the face of the earth. What's really different about Gen Next is how much they're accustomed to constant connectivity, and how they've integrated technology into their everyday lives. To them, the world is virtually borderless. They are not only spending more time online, but the Internet serves as the hub of their lives and everything they do, how they communicate with each other and the world. Smart companies are leveraging online media to make a connection, build trust and engage these younger customer groups. The successful companies have found a way to slip relevant messaging in and become a part of their online activities and an integral part of their lives. Moreover, because these groups are constantly online, they have huge networks of friends and they chat frequently, and are best equipped to generate significant buzz with "word of mouse."

2. Customization. Often referred to as the "entitlement" or "needy" generations, Gen Xers and Ys have grown up hearing Mr. Rogers and their parents telling them how "special" they are. With these groups, Burger's King's old slogan, "Have It Your Way," is taken to the nth degree. These folks can customize any and every thing they can get their hands on. They can design their own footwear online at miadidas.com or nikeID.com, style their own clothing at Landsend.com, configure their own car at mini.com or scion.com and customize their own music playlists for their iPods.

Moreover, if they do business with you, they expect you to know who they are and you'd better demonstrate your appreciation for their patronage or they'll take their business elsewhere – quick. The Internet has offered them instant gratification, and they're accustomed to getting what they want when they want it. They're not fond of hierarchies and having to run things up the flagpole. The Gen X and Y credo: *It's all about me.* To appeal to them, you need to speak their language, personalize their experiences and let them know how much you appreciate their business. If your company can justify the expense, and if you want to keep them, I strongly recommend investing in some form of CRM technology to allow you to reward them for their loyalty and personalize their experiences as much as possible.

Papa John's pizza chain is rolling out a service that lets customers order pizza via text message. Customers first create an account online where they save as many as four different "favorite" orders. Customers can then send a text message at any time using the shorthand "FAV1," "FAV2," "FAV3" or "FAV4."

3. Community. Socializing and sharing personal experiences over the Web is a way of life for younger generations. Pew Research found that at least 54 percent of 18- to 25-year-olds have used a social networking site, and 44 percent have created their own profiles. The face of the Internet has changed to embrace social interactions and provide everyone the chance to have their say. Gen Next customers are vocal about their experiences, too. They're influencing everything from which movies to see to what meals to avoid at specialty restaurants. To attract and engage the Gen X and Y consumers, you need to invite them to the game to play. They are willing to give you raw feedback as long as you're ready for it and provide them with the means to do so. But more important, if they offer you some viable recommendations to improve your product or service delivery, really listen and be open to what they have to say and act on their input. If not, you'll open yourself up to being blasted by the very people you were trying to attract. Companies need to adapt and accept that blogs, podcasts, vodcasts and social networks are here to stay, but they're nothing to be feared. Use them to strengthen your relationship with your future customers.

Deloitte & Touche asked employees to make short videos about their experiences at the accounting firm. The videos were a way of taking social networking and experimenting on how you can use new tools of today to move into a workplace of the future.

One of the biggest setbacks for many people and organizations alike is their unwillingness to change. In order to sustain success in a dynamic environment, it is important to embrace change and adjust accordingly if the market dictates it. In the famous words of Winston Churchill, "There is nothing wrong with change, if it is in the right direction."

CHAPTER 7 FRQs

1. Is your organization too dependent on the baby boomer segment for continued growth?
2. Is your company prepared to make the necessary changes to meet the needs of its future customers?
3. Which is stronger within your organization – its willingness to change or its resistance to it?
4. How difficult will it be for your company to reconsider how it markets its products and services?

Chapter

8

JANE, STOP THIS CRAZY THING!

"Jane, stop this crazy thing!" is a phrase derived from the Hanna-Barbera animated show *The Jetsons,* and best describes this 24/7, quicker, faster, always-on, never-off world we live in today. Whether you realize it or not, we're all part of a spreading epidemic called the "I want it now" syndrome.

This phenomenon is changing the way we work and live; how we communicate with one another; what makes a company successful; and now more than ever how we define a quality customer experience.

What ever happened to "patience is a virtue"? Waiting and downtime are no longer acceptable to today's consumers. Our tolerance for waiting is so low that 23 percent of Americans say they lose patience within five minutes of waiting in line. We just don't have the time to wait anymore. And we don't have to.

Waiting and downtime are no longer acceptable to today's consumers.

The infusion of technology in our lives has provided us with more ways to get things done quicker, cheaper and oftentimes at a higher level of quality than we've ever had before.

What is the most valued currency in the world? It is the dollar? Peso? Yen? Pound? Dinar? None of the above. It's time. And everyone is trying to spend it as efficiently as they possibly can. If your organization is wasting this valued commodity for your customers, you're in danger of losing them because the last thing people have to waste in this crazy world we live in today is time.

The world is a fast and harried place. Dual-income families juggling work, play, kids, soccer games, tackling traffic, you name it. People want stuff that can simplify their lives. As customer service professionals, we should do everything in our power to simplify our customers' lives. That's our job. When we bring difficulty to the customer service experience, we cause frustration for the customer. Businesses forget sometimes why they're in business – to serve customers. Yes, it's that simple. It's common sense. While it may be convenient for a bank to add a gazillion phone prompts to save its bottom line, the customer just wants a solution – quick, fast and in a hurry. Just keep it simple. Take some time to evaluate how you deliver your products and services and see where you can eliminate a process or task to make it easier for your customers to get the answers they seek. Trust me, they'll appreciate it.

It's all about faster, quicker, sooner, I want it now! In a March 2007 online study of 385 executives conducted by Strativity Group, Inc., 85 percent of the respondents report that the demand for speed in interactions is "extremely high" or "high." And 94 percent expect that customer demands for speed and quality will increase over the next three years, with 52 percent expecting a significant increase.

The Internet has drastically squeezed the gap between customer desires and gratification. Customers can find and purchase virtually anything they want in a heartbeat, increasing their expectations for product quality and speedy service. Moreover, it is becoming increasingly challenging for companies to differentiate customer experiences because of the smorgasbord of options available today. When customers are unhappy with a service provider, they can take their business to a competitor at warp speed.

Our desire for speed is rapidly growing into (if it hasn't already become) a full-blown expectation and has significantly impacted the way we deliver products and services today. The days when customers accepted trade-offs between product quality and timeliness of service are over. Satisfying today's customers requires not only that companies deliver high-quality experiences but also that they consistently provide them in a timely manner.

The demand for speed is only going to become more intense as our expectation for speed continues to grow.

Some companies have embraced speed and used it to their advantage. Federal Express' tagline says it loud and clear: "When it absolutely, positively has to be there overnight." Netflix can get DVDs to almost 90 percent of its customers in one business day. GEICO, the car insurance provider, used the cartoon character Speed Racer as a spokesperson and created a tagline that screams speed: "Fifteen minutes could save 15 percent or more on car insurance."

In order to thrive in this "I want it now" culture, organizations first have to acknowledge this shift and then seek out ways to make speed their ally. If businesses don't learn how to accept and embrace speed now, the consequences can be far more damaging in the future, because the demand for speed is not going away. The demand for speed is only going to become more intense as our expectation for speed continues to grow. Companies that are unwilling to face this reality will lose over time because they will fall short of meeting their customers' expectations for speed and quality.

Even Embassy Suites Hotels is getting into the speed game. To meet guests' interest in faster service and more flexible dining options, in January 2008, the chain unveiled a new lobby-based approach to food and beverage service it's calling "Flying Spoons."

Accepting and embracing speed is the first critical step. The most challenging part for many organizations is figuring out what it takes to be successful in this type of business environment and not crash and burn in the process. Below are some things companies should consider when evaluating opportunities to exploit speed to their advantage.

1. Hire for speed. Most organizations searching for the ideal employee often look for candidates who are highly motivated, competitive, dedicated and hard-working. However, what many employees lack is a general passion for helping customers in a timely and efficient manner. Many service employees today have no sense of urgency. Having an innate sense of urgency to take care of the customer is a unique characteristic and skill. Companies wanting to succeed in this "I want it now" culture should seek out (and hire) candidates who possess this invaluable attribute.

2. Release the handcuffs. Organizations should examine the manner in which they deliver their products and services to their customers. I'm sure many of you have witnessed how company procedures and policies can prevent employees from providing the type of fast, high-quality service that customers expect. One example includes having to run routine issues up the flagpole to department managers or supervisors, which oftentimes causes frustration for the customer. While rules are a necessary evil, they should empower all employees so that they can consistently deliver high-quality and speedy service to customers. In addition, organizations should provide their employees with tools that offer customer insight and the ability to customize experiences at every Moment of Impact.

Don't make things more difficult than they need to be. Diffusing a customer service issue as quickly as possible is critical to delivering FRCS. I've found that one of the most frustrating things for customers is having to wait for a solution to their problem.

Customers will continually heighten their expectations for experience, quality and speed of service.

The longer the customer has to wait, the greater the level of frustration. The customer just wants the problem fixed in the least amount of time possible. One of the biggest mistakes many customer service people make is trying to explain the whys for everything. "Well, sir, let me tell you *why* we can't do that here, *why* we can't get you checked in, *why* we can't get your order on time, *why* we couldn't blah, blah, blah, blah." The customer doesn't care about the *whys*. The customer only wants to know *what* you're going to do to fix "my" situation now. Fix the customer's problem as quickly and efficiently as possible.

3. Beware the Zeppelin. Have you ever worked for or with a company that required 4, 7 or even 11 levels of approval for the smallest initiative? In his book *The Age of Speed*, Vince Poscente describes these company types as Zeppelins. Poscente says that Zeppelins proceed at a sloth-like pace and have a tough time maneuvering or changing course quickly. Today, they are obsolete: Zeppelins can't fly fast enough or soar high enough for the age of speed. To thrive in this "I want it now" environment, companies will need to be increasingly responsive and agile, and have the ability (and willingness) to change and adapt when market conditions necessitate it.

4. Don't get too comfortable. Let's not forget that what excites customers today will be tomorrow's yawn. You should be constantly asking yourself the hard question: what innovative touches can we introduce to improve the experience and reduce time and cost for our customers? Successful organizations consistently innovate to maintain their competitive differentiation and preference in the marketplace. Customers will continually heighten their expectations for experience, quality and speed of service. Companies will need to meet those expectations now and in the future to prevent their customers from defecting to the competition.

Identifying and embracing current trends and shifts in the marketplace are critical elements to long-term growth. The most successful companies recognize that the combination of quick service and high-quality, customized experiences is the winning combination to commanding premium pricing, garnering greater share of wallet and increasing customer loyalty.

On my way home one evening, I happened to walk by a Jimmy John's Gourmet Sandwich Shop. In bright red neon, a sign in the window read: "Subs so fast, you'll freak!" You know what? These guys may actually be onto something.

TRADE-OFFS ARE UNACCEPTABLE

Remember the days of old when people were willing to accept trade-offs when it came to fast food? Fast-food restaurants operated under a simple model: as long as you received your food at lightning speed, you would walk away a pretty happy camper. In exchange, customers accepted subpar, preprepared meals that had been sitting under that little lamp for who knows how long. It really didn't matter to fast-food joints if the food tasted like crap. Their M.O. was to get you your meal quick. And customers were willing to accept that trade-off because that was the program. Then, on the other end of the continuum, for those customers who wanted a high-quality, customized dining experience, they would have to wait 30, 45 minutes and even up to an hour or more to receive their meal. That's madness!

My, my, my, how times have changed. Today's customers are no longer willing to accept trade-offs. They want it all. They demand efficiency, quality and personalization to boot. In the last five years, most fast-food places from McDonald's to Taco Bell have improved the level of food quality and how fast they deliver it, and in some instances, they've found ways to offer a basic level of personalization.

Calvin's food for thought:
Customers of today are a lot different from the ones of old. The market has shifted into a new era, a new birth, where today's customers are more educated, more intelligent and all-knowing.

Think about it? Most fast-food joints have a drive-through to save customers time, and McDonald's serves high-quality coffee, fries without trans fat, and Happy Meals with fruit and milk. At Wendy's you can get a loaded baked potato prepared to your liking, and low-fat chicken wraps. And let's not forget, you can choose from more than 19,000 different ways to personalize your coffee at Starbucks.

THE RISE OF THE iCUSTOMER

Today, we live in an "I" society. It's all about how "I" want it. And if you can't make it happen for me, guess what? I'll just go somewhere else and get it! Apple, Inc., has jumped all over this "I" phenomenon in the marketplace with the introduction of several I-based products like the iPhone, iPod and iBook. Well, say hello to the rise of a new generation of consumers I've dubbed iCustomers.

The DNA of iCustomers

1. iCustomers want instant gratification. We live in an "I want it now" economy. The Internet has dramatically intensified the customer's need for speed. Long wait times are no longer acceptable and customers would rather switch to a competitor (with all things being equal) who can satisfy their wants and needs faster. It's nothing personal.

2. iCustomers are smart and savvy. I recall attending one of our Hilton conferences and hearing Tom Keltner, then president of brand management, saying, "Never underestimate the intelligence of your customers. They're a lot smarter than you give them credit for." Customers have tons of information at their fingertips. They know as much about your company as you do, and probably some things you don't.

3. iCustomers decide how (and when) to buy. It's not how you want to sell but how the customer wants to buy. The Internet has shifted the power from sellers to buyers. The most successful companies of the future will be the ones that recognize and embrace this shift. That means delivering products and services to your customers in the way they'd prefer, and looking at how well your company fulfills those wants and needs.

4. iCustomers distinguish marketing hype from reality. In the past, customers believed the ads they saw on television and in print. Customers are skeptical of the product and service claims companies make in the media. Customers are more educated and understand that most consumer ads are more hype than reality. They have the power to bypass traditional marketing channels, and usually do. They derive "real" company truths from their own experiences and those of their friends. Thank goodness for TiVo!

5. iCustomers recognize their worth. Today's customers know how much they mean to your business. They know that so many options in the marketplace exist, and they have no tolerance for poor product and service quality. In essence, if you can't give me what I want when I want it, guess what? I'll just go spend my money with one of your competitors, Perhaps they will recognize and appreciate my worth. No harm, no foul.

6. iCustomers realize "it's all about me." The world revolves around me! YouTube, iPhone, iPod, MySpace, me, me, me, me, me. I want personalization! What can you do for me? This market shift is only going to deepen as customers continually expect more and more customization with their purchases. From the online promotions they receive to simple purchases they make on a routine basis, like music. Heck, today customers can go online and customize a bag of M&M's.

7. iCustomers are brand promiscuous. "If you want loyalty, get a dog!" I saw this headline on the cover of a magazine. Don't be fooled by all the hype. They will cheat on you. Don't assume that because you've got your customers eating out of your hand today, they'll be your customers for life. They might stick around as long as you don't screw up or if nothing better comes along (which is practically every day). These folks will accept your invitation to be a loyal customer, along with two or three of your competitors. How many hotel frequency programs do *you* belong to?

8. iCustomers are the new influencers. With the proliferation of social media, today your customers possess the power to make or break you. Blogs, chat rooms, and other social media are outweighing the impact traditional marketing has on consumer purchasing behavior. Never underestimate their power of influence.

CHAPTER 8 FRQs

1. Does your company hire people who have an innate sense of urgency?
2. Has your company embraced the customer's need for speed in today's marketplace?
3. Have your given your line-level employees the autonomy to resolve customer issues in a timely manner?
4. How many layers of approval are necessary to make simple decisions within your organization?
5. What is your company doing today to address the emerging needs of the iCustomer?
6. Does your company look for new ways to build efficiencies within its operations?

Chapter

9

YOU'RE FIRED! IT'S NOT JUST DONALD'S TAGLINE ANYMORE

During a conference in Orlando, I hooked up for dinner with a good friend of mine named Kyle. During our conversation he told me a story that I just have to share with you. He said that he had just sat down for dinner and a movie one Saturday evening when the telephone rang at about 5:30. It was his homeowner's insurer, Allstate, calling to say they were dropping him in November. "I'm not really upset about them dumping me, but that they would call me on a Saturday evening to do it. Now that's cold," he said. Being the customer service fanatic that I am, I got a little peeved hearing Kyle's story. I've heard of insurance companies dumping customers for filing too many claims, but he pointed out to me that he hadn't filed a claim since Allstate began insuring his home in 1995. After conducting my own investigation, I found out that Allstate stopped under- writing new homeowners insurance in Florida in 2005. When the dust clears, the state's third-largest property insurer will ultimately drop about 375,000 customers.

Apparently, my buddy Kyle is not the only person to fall victim to the customer-firing epidemic. In late July 2007, Sprint-Nextel sent about 1,000 of its 53 million customers a personal "Dear John" letter. Why? Those people had called their contact center an average of 25 times a month with the same problems, a rate 40 times higher than average customers. So Sprint "fired" them! When news got out about Sprint's customer-dumping strategy, message boards started popping up online everywhere urging Sprint customers to cancel their service to demonstrate their discontent. Their major competitors, AT&T and Verizon, immediately released statements saying they would not follow suit because they cared about all of their customers.

In April 2007, guess which company earned the number one spot in MSN Money's Customer Service Hall of Shame? That's right, Sprint-Nextel. According to MSN's study of more than 5,000 respondents, a remarkable 40 percent of people who had an opinion of Sprint's customer service said it was "poor." I know what you're thinking. How could a company with such poor customer service have the audacity to fire its customers? What the heck is going on here? Businesses firing customers? I've always been taught that *the customer is always right* and that *every customer is valuable.*

"Be a leader on quality or price, but don't get stuck in the middle."
Steve Ridgway, Chief Executive of Virgin Atlantic

Sprint was basically firing a handful of customers who spent an excessive amount of time complaining about the same problems to reduce service costs while making it easier for customers with legitimate issues to get through to customer service. On the surface, Sprint's firing strategy may seem cold, callous and contrary to everything we've learned about *always putting the customer first.* Not if Sprint's plan was to improve customer service levels and strengthen relationships with their customers over the long haul.

What led Sprint to make such a decision? If those 1,000 customers keep calling with the same problems over and over, we can conclude that they were not happy with Sprint, and Sprint was not happy trying to serve them with little success. It's apparent that this relationship wasn't working out. So Sprint felt it was better to end the relationship than let it drag out when both parties knew it was over. Sound familiar to anyone?

Unprofitable customers can be a big problem for businesses. Being able to identify them and make them more profitable can be critical to your company's success. But sometimes, even the best efforts fail. In that case, the best solution is to show problem customers to the door in a way that doesn't create more issues for your company. So how do you decide who goes and who stays?

1. Separate the wheat from the chaff. First, consider your existing customer base and identify who your "best customers" are. Most companies have gobs of information about their customers that they have never mined. Consider criteria like revenue, profitability, levels of repeat business, service cost, price sensitivity, etc. Most important, everyone has to agree on the selection criteria that best suit your organization. After completion of this exercise, you may discover that you're investing more than you'd like on some customers who aren't producing the ROI you anticipated.

2. Find out why they buy from you. Determine why these "best customers" buy from you and not your competitors. Identify what's important to them, what attracted them to you in the first place, what they would like to see you do better and, more important, how you could do more business with them. Is your company known for offering rock-bottom prices or personalized service? Trying to accomplish both could pull your company in opposite directions and drive away the customers you need to keep. In a recent *Wall Street*

Journal article, Steve Ridgway, chief executive of Virgin Atlantic, stated, "Be a leader on quality or price, but don't get stuck in the middle."

3. Laser beam your efforts. Profile the type of customers you want to do business with, identify their buying habits, industry sector, size and needs. You want to mirror the profile as close to your "best customers" as possible. Focus your sales and marketing efforts on these target customers. You might even consider offering some sort of incentive to get them in the door. However, fight off the temptation to discount your services. Although that's the simplest and most obvious route to take, discounting will hurt your business in the long term.

4. Fire your worst customers. As for the non-profitable customers, consider reducing your reliance on them and then eventually eliminating them from your portfolio. I'm not advocating calling these folks up tomorrow and giving them the boot. First, look at how you might be able to turn them into profitable customers. If you determine that the relationship isn't working out and firing them is the only option, remember that maintaining your company's reputation is very important. Offer a solution. Consider unloading the fired customers on a competitor. If it all works out well, these customers may think you did them a favor.

Today, we live in a highly competitive marketplace and the customer experience will make or break a company. Nobody wants to be known as the company that fires its customers. On the other hand, if firing some customers allows you to devote more time to your best customers, and leads to increased profitability and customer satisfaction, then a "Dear John" letter today could be the pathway to marital bliss tomorrow if delivered with a customer-centric focus.

CHAPTER 9 FRQs

1. Does your company know who its best and most profitable customers are?
2. Do you know why your best customers buy from you?
3. What buying factors does your company "own" in its market space?
4. Are your company's sales and marketing efforts targeted to your best customers?
5. Does your company waste too much time and money on unprofitable customers?

Chapter

10

ARE DISENGAGED EMPLOYEES SINKING YOUR BUSINESS?

Have you ever thought about what happens to the customer experience between the time an employee considers leaving your company and when the actual event occurs? Scary thought? I agree. Employee disengagement is a process that can take days, weeks, months or even years until the actual decision to leave occurs.

I read a disturbing statistic in *Business Week* a couple of years ago. In a job satisfaction survey of 5,000 households, 25 percent of workers said they were "just showing up to collect a paycheck." Only 14 percent said that they were very satisfied with their job. Ouch!

The Gallup Organization estimates that there are 22 million actively disengaged employees who cost the American economy up to $350 billion per year in lost productivity, including absence, illness and other problems that result when workers are unhappy at work. Not to mention the potentially lost revenue from customers who never return because they encountered a disengaged employee.

We would be foolish to ignore this important fact: if employees are not engaged with the work they do, it will play out loud and clear in the customer experience. All of us have experienced this tragic phenomenon at one time or another. First, we have the bank teller who pretends he can't see you standing in line. Then we have the reservation agent who exudes the passion of a doorknob. Let's not forget the angry call center rep who makes you feel guilty for imposing on her precious time. These employees are essentially "checked out." They're sleepwalking through their workday, just putting in time, not energy or passion into their work.

As customers, we appreciate and immediately recognize an engaged employee. Engaged employees perform with passion and feel a profound connection to the companies they work for. They routinely produce significantly more than the job requires; focus on getting things right the first time; search for new ways to improve things; encourage co-workers to higher levels of performance; and embrace rather than resist change.

According to an article in *1to1* magazine, in an effort to engage its 15,000 employees in a more customer-centric culture, GE Capital Solutions launched a company-wide campaign called *In Their Shoes*, which asked employees to put themselves in the shoes of customers when doing their jobs. Each employee received a shoe box with the *In Their Shoes* logo on it. The box contained a copy of *The Ultimate Question* by Net Promoter Score co-creator Fred Reichheld and *In Their Shoes* note cards to encourage listing or sharing information about customer-based successes. The note cards are also used to congratulate colleagues on a job well done.

The program also included a contest that recognized and rewarded employees who demonstrated exceptional customer focus. More than 700 people were nominated by their peers with 13 winners selected. An e-mail announcing the 13 winners included a link to a portal that featured a profile and story on each of the winners. Four grand prize winners received a four-day getaway of their choice, and the runners-up received a $500 American Express gift check.

At the end of the day, GE Capital Solutions still lives by the numbers. And those numbers demonstrated that the company's approach worked. Its 2005 $1.5 billion profit jumped to $1.8 billion in 2006.

MY TWO RIGHT FEET

My momma used to always tell me, "Boy, always have on a nice pair of shoes. Shoes say something about a man." It made sense to me, so I always made sure that I kept on a nice pair of shoes. It was Thursday afternoon and I was packing to leave for a presentation I had to conduct on Friday morning in Chicago. I was getting ready to pack my shoes and noticed that they looked pretty beat up. I can put some wear and tear on a pair of shoes. For those people who have witnessed one of my presentations, they'll confirm that I'm a real maniac on the platform. And those shoes had seen their share of presentations to say the least. "I can buy some new shoes when I hit Chicago," I thought, so I decided to leave them behind. I was staying downtown and finding a shoe store wouldn't be a problem. Deciding on which one, though? That's a whole different story. I checked into the Marriott, got settled into my room and then at about 6:30 p.m. I headed out to Michigan Avenue to begin my shoe quest.

Shopping is not a favorite task of mine, so after about the fourth store, I began to think about throwing in the towel and then at about 7:45 it happened. I looked into the window of a Cole Haan shoe store and saw THE PAIR. Hallelujah! The store was scheduled to close at 8 o'clock, so I dashed in like a kid into a candy store and asked the salesperson as I pointed to the shoes in the window, "Do you have those in a 10½?" "Let me check."

He walked into the back and returned with a box. He took off the lid and there they were. The shoes came in a pair of nice cloth bags – very nice touch. He took one out and proceeded to place it on my right foot as I sat on the couch. The salesperson was really a nice guy and I was impressed with his sense of humor. I tried on the right shoe and it felt great. I told him to pack 'em up. I left the store absolutely ecstatic about my shiny new pair of shoes.

"Dude you're going to be sharp tomorrow morning," I thought to myself. I got back to the room, walked over to the closet and pulled out my black suit, held up my new shoes against it in the full-length mirror, and that's when I realized something strange about my new kicks. I couldn't believe my eyes! I had two right shoes!!! It was about 8:30 and the shoe store had closed at 8:00. My presentation was at 10:30 the next morning. The store didn't open until 10:00 a.m. I started panicking and sweating profusely. I called the store to see if they were still open. The phone rang about five times. Thank goodness my salesperson answered. I explained my dilemma and he immediately apologized. He told me that he would stay there until I came back and he would give me a left shoe.

When I got back to the store, he locked the door behind me and asked me to walk over to the counter because he needed my signature. We exchanged shoes and he chuckled. I told you he had a sense of humor. Here's the kicker. He goes, "Mr. Stovall, we're really sorry about what happened, so we'd like to give you the left shoe on us. The adjustment has already been applied to your credit card." Now that was very cool. This situation taught me two very important lessons. One, never leave the house without a good-looking pair of shoes; and two, smart companies walk in the shoes of their customers. I love you, Cole Haan!

In 2004, Hewitt Associates in Lincolnshire, Illinois, tracked about 300 companies over a five-year period and found that increases in employee engagement clearly preceded improvements in financial performance. Even among those companies with below-average profit, a positive change in employee attitude tended to precede a profit increase.

Another three-year study of 41 employers by Towers-Perrin-ISR found companies that worked consistently on engaging their employees saw a 3.74 percent increase in operating profit over a three-year period, while companies with poorly engaged employees actually experienced a 2 percent decline. Both study results demonstrate how an engaged workforce can positively impact the bottom line.

Keeping your employees engaged is essential to your company's future success. Great companies achieve sustainable growth and profits because they do what other companies fail to do – they keep their employees actively engaged and leverage the individual strengths and talents of their employees to better connect with their customers.

1. Prep employees for success. Employees need to clearly understand what is expected of them. Managers need to give employees a big-picture view of how their roles contribute to the overall customer experience and the future growth of the company. Make sure employees have everything they need to do their jobs with excellence. Place them in their strength zones. Make sure they have personal development opportunities for continued growth. Employees stay actively engaged when their jobs are kept exciting and challenging.

2. Champion employee input. At GE, more than 20 times during 2006, employees were asked to attend small group meetings to tackle specific customer issues. One of these groups produced process improvements that increased construction business revenue by more than 40 percent.

Remember, you're only as good as the people who report to you.

Another generated 12 ideas for organizational growth in 2007. As a result, six of the ideas will be implemented. At Northwest Airlines, about 50 employee involvement teams have been formed to look at everything from improving luggage performance to saving fuel and choosing new uniforms for customer contact workers.

3. Promote and reward candor. Candor gets more people engaged in ongoing business decisions. Absence of candor blocks smart ideas and quick action. It hinders great employees from contributing everything they have to offer to a company. Foster and cultivate an environment where employees are encouraged to participate in innovation and making the company better. In his recent book entitled *Winning*, Jack Welch says, "Even though candor is vital to winning, it is hard to instill in any group, no matter what size. But is can be done. To get candor, you reward it, praise it and talk about it."

4. Keep your antennae attuned. It's critical that you stay actively engaged in your business. Remain close to the action and spend some time on the front lines. Just as marketplace and customer needs change, so do your employees' needs. The challenge for managers develops when the first signs of disengaging appear in an engaged employee. The symptoms need to be quickly addressed. Don't ignore the shift in behavior hoping things will just get better. Without intervention this behavior is likely to continue in a downward spiral. In most instances, the disengagement process can be interrupted by having a meaningful conversation with the employee. Remember, you're only as good as the people who report to you. Great managers invest more time with their most productive and talented people because they have the most potential.

Calvin's food for thought:
Nothing can be more detrimental to a service organization than a growing segment of disengaged customers.

FIRST IMPRESSIONS ARE LASTING IMPRESSIONS

Remember the old adage, *you never get a second chance to make a first impression*? Make sure that your employees deliver on what your company promises every day. How many times have you visited or called a company for the first time and were met by a rude receptionist or contact center rep? What happened? I'd guess that you left or never called back. However, it's not that easy when you're dealing with cable companies. Sadly, consumers have limited choices when it comes to cable, so in most instances, you're forced to deal with their incompetence. I can talk about cable companies all day long, but I don't want to get sidetracked, so I'll move on. What many organizations fail to understand is that first-time customers will not return if their first experience with your company is negative. Therefore, every contact with the customer needs to be taken seriously. And everything counts: how promptly your phones are answered; how welcomed your customers feel when they walk through your doors; how quickly you respond to your customers' needs. Every employee on the team needs to understand how important they are to ensuring that a positive first impression is conveyed at all times – no exceptions.

YOU CAN'T TRAIN FOR PASSION

Don't you love to do business with companies that are passionate about what they do? I don't mean to sound cynical, but it's so hard to find passionate people in companies today. Aren't you sick and tired of going to business establishments to spend your hard-earned money only to be confronted with a bank teller, customer service rep, desk clerk or fast-food employee who couldn't care less? Where's the passion?

You can't train people to have passion. Don't waste your time trying.

When I was front desk clerk at Holiday Inn City Centre in downtown Chicago, I was one of the best. I was truly passionate about it. When you are a desk clerk, you never know what a guest is going to ask of you at any given moment. I prided myself on being the go-to person for things. I knew where all of the downtown landmarks were, how long it took to get there, the restaurants, the best pizza places, you name it. I knew Chicago and I was proud of that. My passion did not come from training – it came from an inner drive to be the best desk clerk I could possibly be.

You can't train people to have passion. Don't waste your time trying. I'm a big proponent of being yourself and responding to customer needs based on your gut. I believe people do need training on the do's and don'ts, but when it comes to delivering a positive customer experience, either you have it or you don't.

Calvin's food for thought:
Whether the employee has face-to-face customer contact or they work in a contact center, being passionate is nothing you can train people for. Either they have it or they don't. Plain and simple.

My younger brother Kevin supervises the door and bellman staff at a Residence Inn hotel in downtown Chicago. During the summer of 2006, my wife and I took a trip to the Windy City and we stayed at his hotel. One morning I came down to the hotel lobby to enjoy my complimentary breakfast and spend some time with my brother while he was working. This was during a very busy period for the hotel, and there were people all over the lobby. I took a seat on a bench outside in front of the hotel to get some air. Kevin and one other bellman were on a roll that day, and I watched my brother as he moved at the speed of light! He was parking cars, picking up cars, escorting guests to their rooms and checking luggage. He was very knowledgeable about Chicago landmarks, and customers were bombarding him with questions at every turn. This dude was all over the place! And through it all, he kept on the brightest smile and a genuine customer service attitude most organizations would kill to have just a fraction of their employees exhibit. He was passionate about his role and what it meant to deliver a memorable experience.

That's fanatically relentless customer service! As you could imagine, I felt so proud to be his big brother. Kevin, you're the MAN!

CHAPTER 10 FRQs

1. How many disengaged employees do you think your company has on staff?
2. Does your company tend to hold on to disengaged employees too long? Why?
3. Do your employees know how important their roles are to the customer experience?
4. Are your employees solicited for their feedback and encouraged to provide input on company initiatives?
5. Are your employees celebrated and praised for being up-front about service deficiencies?
6. How much time do *you* spend on the front lines?
7. What do *you* do when you find out a valued A-player on your team is unhappy?
8. Are *you* spending too much time with disengaged employees and not enough time with your A/B players?

Chapter 11

SERVICE RECOVERY MALFUNCTION AND THE BAKED POTATO

My wife loves baked potatoes, especially with a good steak. One evening we decided to have dinner at this steak house in downtown Minneapolis. When we arrived, a pleasant hostess greeted us and proceeded to escort us to our table. After we had sat there for about ten minutes or so, a hurried waiter finally arrived – not to take our order, but to complain about how short staffed they were. He brought over two glasses of water, handed us two menus and then dashed off. About ten minutes later, he came back to take our orders. My wife ordered an eight-ounce filet and her side dish – a baked potato with all the fixins. I then placed my order. About 20 minutes later the waiter came back and said to my wife, "We're out of baked potatoes." *Uh oh, folks, here we go.*

My wife replied, "Why didn't you tell me that before now?" His response, "I forgot." My wife said, "What a bummer. I really wanted a baked potato with my steak." He replied, "Well, if you're willing to wait another 15 minutes we can get you one." Mind you, we'd already been sitting there for more than 30 minutes. "I thought you didn't have any baked potatoes," said my wife. "Well, they're not ready to come out. They need to be put in the oven and prepared," said the waiter. "Fine, I'll wait," she responded. Now here comes the real doozy: "We've already prepared both your steaks, so it would be better if you selected another side item or your steak is going to sit until the potato is done." My wife asked, "Why don't you just fix me another steak?" "I can't do that," the waiter replied. As you can imagine, my wife was getting a little miffed by then. "What do you mean you can't do that? If you had told me from the beginning you didn't have any baked potatoes, I would have made another selection. And now you're telling me that in order to have a baked potato, the trade-off for me is a cold steak?" The waiter said, "I understand, but I don't have the authority to do that. I'd have to ask my manager." Of course, we replied to him in unison, "Go ask your manager." He again dashed off. After about five minutes, he returned and said, "My manager said it's okay to fix you another steak." Then he turned to me: "Sir, are you okay eating your dinner right now?" My reply to him was an exasperated, "No problem. As long as this works out for you. We're just customers." For the next 15 minutes, my wife watched me eat my dinner. They blew it. It was obvious to me that service recovery was not a priority at this restaurant. As my momma used to say, "Common sense ain't all too common sometimes."

Service recovery is simply restoring a customer's positive feelings about a company after a bad experience and taking action to resolve the problem. It's what separates the best from the rest. Service recovery is more than complaint handling. Service recovery is all about turning a problem into a positive for both the customer and the company. Simply put, it's resolving a customer's problem and sending that person out the door excited about doing business with you. It's about turning a bad experience from *tragic* to *magic*.

"It is not how satisfied you keep your customers, it's how many satisfied customers you keep."
Fred Reichheld, author of *The Ultimate Question*

Research has shown that customers who have had an issue resolved effectively through a company's service recovery actions are in fact more loyal than those who have not had a problem. Effective service recovery practices lead to customer retention. Think about your own personal experiences when you had a service or product letdown. Did the company apologize for the mishap, offer you a quick resolution and perhaps compensate you for the inconvenience? If so, weren't you more likely to buy from that company again because of the confidence you now had in their business practices?

One of the most effective ways to improve your company's service reputation is to perfect your recovery process. Service recovery creates positive word of mouth and minimizes the bad press that the absence of service recovery practices can create. Customers are impressed by companies that make a conscious effort to recover when customers have received a lower quality of service than they expected. Having a service recovery process clearly communicates to your customers that you value their business and will stand behind your product or service, regardless of the circumstances.

THE TRIPLE-A SERVICE RECOVERY PROCESS

Do you have a service recovery process in place at your company? Service recovery practices are a critical element in any organization, but they don't just happen. The culture must be ready for service recovery since employees must embrace it, own it and drive it.

1. Apologize for the mistake. If you don't apologize and make customers feel like you really care, it's very difficult to recover the customer afterward. Actively listen to the customer, show empathy and demonstrate that you sincerely care about what happened. Not just a quick and robotic "I'm sorry," but a real acknowledgment of the mistake and a genuine apology to make the customer know that you are being sincere. First error: the waiter never apologized for his mistake.

2. Accept responsibility for the mistake. No excuses. Take full responsibility for the customer's problem. The customer needs to trust that you will resolve the problem. Blaming someone else or another department is unacceptable. If you can't take care of the problem right away, tell your customer that you will research and resolve the problem. Once a trust-destroying mistake happens, piling any type of deception on top of it will probably ruin any chance of recovery. While it's critical to take responsibility, be careful not to disguise it in any way, and don't "spin" your story. When the waiter arrived at our table, he blamed our long wait on a staff shortage. Bad move.

3. Act quickly to resolve the mistake. Act promptly. After-the-fact offers to fix a problem are next to meaningless. The idea is to fix the problem as swiftly as possible to the customer's satisfaction, not the company's. If you are going to attempt service recovery by offering some form of compensation, it needs to be something that is truly of use to the customer. If you come up with compensation schemes to minimize the direct cost to the company, you are bound to offer something of little value to the customer. Also be careful to not overpromise, because that will do more harm than good. The restaurant manager offered us a free dinner on our next visit. That's okay, but he should have comped my wife's dinner and then offered a free dinner certificate. Perhaps we would have considered returning.

To sum it up, the front line is the bottom line. Our waiter friend had to get a manager's approval to cook another steak. Employee empowerment and ongoing problem-resolution training are the backbone of service recovery. At Zappos.com, each rep is empowered to do whatever is necessary to satisfy the customer. If a customer receives a defective shoe, the rep can just replace it rather than escalate the issue to a manager. Employees must have the autonomy to do whatever it takes to make the customer happy, on the spot. Yes, we do need to institute policies and procedures, but I encourage you to give your employees some room to make decisions about how to serve the customer. Poor handling of a customer issue, as we read in our baked potato story, will just exacerbate dissatisfaction and lead to lost customers.

THE POWER OF EMPOWERMENT

How many times have you heard and seen the words "employee empowerment" over the past ten years? Too many to count, right? Now how many times have you actually seen empowerment exercised at service organizations? Let me guess . . . about as often as you'd see a glass of ice water in hell. Maybe that's a little over the top, but sadly, we're still dealing with the same crap we dealt with years ago when it comes to a customer issue. We still get the same robotic response: "I need to check with my manager." Team leaders, remember one important reality: you're only as good as the people you surround yourself with. Why? It's simple: you can't do it all. You can't be everywhere at all times. You must relinquish some of that great power you possess. You have to empower your employees to handle customer problems. More important, they must be given the proper tools to effectively handle customer problems when they do arise.

What really drives customer loyalty? Is it price? Is it how you interact with your customers?

In *The Nordstrom Way,* business writer Robert Spector recounts the story of the misguided customer who took back a set of tires to a Nordstrom store in Alaska. The tires were graciously accepted by the salesperson, even though the Seattle-based fashion retailer did not sell – and has never sold – automobile tires. That simple yet fanatically relentless act truly demonstrates the essence of employee empowerment.

IT'S NOT JUST ABOUT THE CHICKEN SANDWICH

Have you ever eaten at a Chik-fil-A restaurant? If you haven't, you are missing out on one of the finer things in life. For those of you who have, you know exactly what I'm talking about, right? Chik-fil-A restaurants are primarily concentrated in the Southeast. This place served as one of my favorite joints to have lunch during my days at Hilton. Their restaurants are always clean, employees are always welcoming and friendly and not to mention, they make a mean chicken sandwich – actually one of the best.

It's not just about the chicken sandwich – it's about the experience.

When we were living in Memphis, I recall one evening when my wife came home raving about an incident that happened to her at Chick-fil-A. She was on her way to work that morning and decided to stop by the neighborhood Chick-fil-A drive-through to get a tasty chicken biscuit sandwich. When she pulled up to the pay window, to her surprise she saw that she'd forgotten her purse at home. The young lady in the window realized my wife's dilemma and said, "That's okay, ma'am, I have mornings like that myself. Please take the sandwich and bring us the money the next time you're in the neighborhood." WOW! That response blew my wife's mind. Today, if you ask her about Chick-fil-A, she won't even talk about their wonderful chicken sandwiches anymore. What she *will* talk about is the Chick-fil-A "no purse" experience. As you could imagine, she's told her friends, relatives, colleagues, neighbors and anyone else who'll listen to her story. She is a bona fide Chick-fil-A advocate! Loyalty relies on customers making a connection beyond the transaction. And guess where we have to stop and have a bite every time we visit our family in Memphis? You guessed it. Remember my friends, it's not just about the chicken sandwich – it's about the experience.

Your employees need to be empowered to take care of customers and create positive Moments of Impact, especially when those unexpected circumstances arise.

1. Don't talk about it. *Be* about it. Once and for all, give your team members the power to become customer service heroes! Empower your line-level employees to take care of the customer. Customer frustrations increase when line-level employees aren't given the proper authority to take care of problems. Ensure that your employees have been properly trained, and provide them with the tools to take care of customer issues. Having been in the service industry for as long as I have,

I'm baffled at how many establishments still haven't gotten this simple concept down. Of course, there will be some things that require management approval. But in most instances, 90 percent of problems can be immediately resolved by a competent, knowledgeable line-level employee.

Just do what you promise.

---

2. Deliver on what you promise. I've witnessed in so many instances front-line employees making promises to customers that they simply can't (and didn't) deliver on. My momma always used to say to me, "Boy, don't let your mouth write a check your behind can't cash." Don't overpromise—unless you're going to make it happen. This is one the biggest mistakes service organizations make. When your employees tell a customer that they are going to do something, the customer expects it to happen. Once it comes out of the employee's mouth, it then becomes their responsibility to deliver on it. The ball is now in their court. If they drop the ball – it's game over. At this point it doesn't matter what their excuse is. All they've done is set themselves up to let the customer down. The Nike tagline *Just Do It* applies here. If you promise to call someone on a particular day, just do it. If you promise to deliver a product on a certain day, just do it.

The "customer is always right" and other sticky phrases like it suggest that a company will do *everything* the customer requests. In my opinion, that's unrealistic and I don't believe you can do this 100 percent of the time. What I do believe is that *every* situation is negotiable as long as you offer the customer some options. That's how you create a win-win. Just do what you promise.

CHAPTER 11 FRQs

1. Does your company have a Service Recovery Process in place? Is it in writing?
2. When something falls through the cracks, does your company (and its employees) resolve the issue to the customer's satisfaction or the company's?
3. Are your employees truly empowered to make decisions on the front lines or are they punished for breaking the rules in order to meet customer needs?

Chapter

12

THE IMPLODE EFFECT AND ITS IMPACT ON YOUR BOTTOM LINE

In summer 2007, I redeemed some of my American Express reward points for a $100 gift certificate off my car rental purchase. Following an uneventful flight to Chicago, I eagerly headed down to the lower level at Midway Airport to grab my baggage and pick up my rental car.

When I arrived at the facility, there were three people already in line. Two employees, one of whom was a trainee, were taking care of customers. Then there was a third person at the other end of the counter, ticking away on a computer. She never looked up. She just kept on tick, tick, tick, tick, tick, ticking away. About five minutes went by and three more people joined us in line. After standing there for another 10 minutes or so, it was obvious that these service agents were having some challenges. I watched the trainee walk over to the young lady at the end of the counter to ask her a question. The young lady grudgingly glanced up at the trainee and snapped her response. After the trainee walked away, the young lady gave the line a fleeting look, put her head back down and began to tick, tick, tick, tick, tick away. I turned around and the line was now about ten people deep.

While most companies will look at the many external factors affecting their business, many fail to look inside for possible customer service deficiencies.

After about 30 minutes, I finally reached the service counter. I got the trainee. I could immediately tell by the expression on her face she was having a rough day. Yes, I wanted to yell at her, but I couldn't – she was a trainee for God's sake. I'm not that heartless. We went through the formalities and then I said the magic words, "I have a $100 gift certificate." It was like she was staring into the face of Medusa. I watched as her body turned into stone. She replied, "Excuse me, sir. I need to ask my supervisor how to enter this certificate." My immediate response: "Please tell me that's not the supervisor down there." I looked down the counter and there she was, head down, tick, tick, tick, tick, tick, ticking away. The trainee walked over. The supervisor looked up from her computer, snatched the certificate and quickly sashayed down to the computer in front of me. She didn't say one word, proceeded to do her thing, looked at the trainee and said, "There you go." She glanced at the line, walked back to her computer – tick, tick, tick, tick, tick, ticking away. I couldn't believe it. I could hear the grumbling coming from the people in line getting louder and louder. I wouldn't have been shocked if the trainee had told the supervisor to take that job and shove it and never returned. The Implode Effect in action.

Merriam-Webster's online definition of the word "implode" is: 1 : to burst inward. 2 : to collapse inward; *also* : to become greatly reduced as if from collapsing. 3 : to break down or fall apart from within.

If you can't get it right on the inside, how do you expect to get it right on the outside?

While most companies will look at the many external factors affecting their business, many fail to look inside for possible customer service deficiencies. Poor internal customer service leads to decreased productivity and low employee morale, not to mention the ongoing inter-departmental frustrations that ultimately impact the bottom line.

IT'S WHAT'S INSIDE THAT COUNTS

Internal customer service is defined as the level of service you provide to your colleagues within your organization, as well as to vendors or anyone one else you rely on to get your job done. You haven't seen much about internal customer service lately, but it is vitally important to an organization's ongoing success. If you can't get it right on the inside, how do you expect to get it right on the outside? Your internal customers need to feel the love too! Your employees are so critical to the success of your company. It disheartens me when I hear and see companies not taking care of the ones who help make their customers happy.

Your internal customers need to feel the love too!

Below are some tips to help you improve the level of internal customer service within your company and steer clear of the Implode Effect.

1. Change your perspective. View your colleagues as internal customers – not as nuisances. Try looking at their "legitimate" interruptions as opportunities to help them out. When a colleague visits your office with a true request, give the speaker the floor and your full attention. Giving the speaker your undivided attention assures that you're focused on the matter at hand, reducing the probability of unclear expectations and problems later on down the road.

2. Exercise the basics. Dependability, responsiveness and consistency. These are the underlying principles to delivering exceptional customer service to external customers, and they should carry the same weight for your internal customers. You want your internal customers to feel confident and assured that when they come to you (or your department) for help, they are going to always receive high-quality work in a timely and consistent manner.

3. Make things clear. The primary factor leading to most dissatisfied or unhappy internal customers is unclear expectations. In short, the service provider wasn't clear on what, when or why he or she was supposed to deliver a product or service. Before the service provider walks out of your office or meeting, ensure that they are clear on your expectations, including timing, follow-up, end results, and other issues.

4. Manage your time. Make sure that you are being sensitive to your service provider's other commitments and giving them sufficient time to complete your request. Most people understand that "emergencies" arise from time to time. However, all of your requests shouldn't be so-called emergencies. That practice demonstrates a lack of respect for the other person's schedule and leads to unwanted conflict. Your poor time management skills shouldn't become your service provider's emergency.

5. Break free of silos. In his book *Silos, Politics and Turf Wars*, Patrick Lencioni talks about how the concept of "silos" has become synonymous with the barriers that separate work teams, departments and divisions, causing people who are supposed to be on the same team to work against one another. Spend some time with other departments to learn how you can improve communication and processes. You're all on the same team, customers of one another, and dependent upon one another.

While these tips are not all that a company can do to enhance the level of internal customer service, they do offer some things to think about for those companies who fail to turn their customer service practices inside out to answer some critical questions to their ongoing customer experience woes. Remember, it's what's inside that truly counts.

CHAPTER 12 FRQs

1. Do your employees treat each other as internal customers?
2. Do your employees display the same level of urgency for internal requests and service needs as they do for external customers?
3. Do silos and communication barriers within your company negatively impact the quality of internal customer service within your organization?

Chapter

13

SHOW 'EM THE LOVE!

In the previous chapter, I talked about the importance of internal customer service and why getting it right on the inside is critical to delivering a positive experience for your external customers. Customer Service Week presents the perfect opportunity to celebrate and demonstrate how much you value the customer service champions who make those experiences come to life for your customers on a day-to-day basis. The International Customer Service Association began Customer Service Week in 1988. In 1992 the U.S. Congress proclaimed Customer Service Week a nationally recognized event, celebrated annually during the first full week of October (to learn more about Customer Service Week, visit www.icsa.com/csweek.)

Whether your organization decides to celebrate for one day or for an entire week, I've listed six tips on how to get your CS Week celebration on its way:

1. Fire them up. Hand out buttons and send out teaser e-mails to build energy and excitement and get the buzz going. Decorate the customer service department and the entire company with CSW posters banners and balloons early to generate excitement for the coming celebration.

2. Run with the theme. Incorporate the year's CS Week theme as the foundation for your events and activities during the celebration. Incorporating games, challenges and contests is an excellent method for enhancing teamwork, reducing stress and building camaraderie among the team members.

3. Throw a party. Start the week with a kickoff celebration. Pizza parties are an excellent way to demonstrate to your customer service champions how much you appreciate what they do. Invite senior management to the party to mingle with the team. Consider inviting a different senior manager each day of the week to visit the department and discuss how vital customer service is to the organization's success.

4. Praise them. During the week, distribute service awards and certificates on key measures like number of positive customer comments, number of calls handled, conversion rates, and so on. Create some humorous awards to add some laughs and lighten up the crew. Give out small prizes like movie passes, Starbucks, Blockbuster and fast-food gift certificates, CDs, or iTunes gift cards. I don't need to tell you that cash is always well received. Be creative with your prizes. Remember, it's the thought that counts.

5. Invest in their growth. Consider inviting some outside vendors to come in and deliver professional development seminars and training on hot topics like personal presence, how to avoid burnout, reducing stress, work-life balance, handling irate customers, career development and other areas of interest.

6. Make it happen. Share the responsibility of putting together a CS Week celebration. Form a CSW planning committee of customer service reps to assist in creating an activity for each day. The idea here is to do something to demonstrate how much you appreciate their contribution to the organization's success. Don't make things more difficult than they need be. Just keep it simple and fun for all.

CHAPTER FRQs

1. What programs does your company currently have in place to show appreciation for your employees' contributions?
2. Are *you* actively praising, coaching and mentoring employees on a frequent basis?
3. What are *you* doing to ensure that your employees feel appreciated and valued?

Chapter

14

IS GREAT SERVICE BURNING A HOLE IN YOUR POCKET?

Gateway originally sold its personal computer products solely through direct channels. Faced with eroding market share, management decided to address a major concern in high-tech markets – customers' lack of technical expertise and knowledge. Their solution would be to provide more personal attention and hand-holding for customers. To do this, the company decided to enter the retail market. When Gateway's new stores opened in 1996, they were nothing short of spectacular. Store employees were sharp and supportive, and the employee-to-customer ratio was pretty high compared to normal standards. They had top-notch education materials, and the stores were strategically located to ensure heavy foot traffic. Gateway had succeeded in bringing customers at all levels of expertise through its doors.

Today's smart companies recognize that the new M.O. is to serve customers better, faster, cheaper and to make more money in the process.

Then we fast-forward to April 2004, when the company closed the last of more than 300 stores. How could this have happened? Gateway had figured out a solution to a major customer concern. Unfortunately for Gateway, the approach it took was too expensive. Moreover, the company didn't anticipate that customers wouldn't be willing to pay a premium for all that personal attention. Sadly, customers took their newly acquired information out the door and placed orders with one of Gateway's lower-priced competitors. Ouch! If Gateway had only asked the right questions up front, it would have realized how important price (and personalized service) was to its customers.

Author Frances X. Frei describes this tragic story in her 2006 *Harvard Business Review* article, "Breaking the Trade-Off Between Efficiency and Service."

Today's smart companies recognize that the new M.O. is to serve customers better, faster, cheaper and to make more money in the process. But the reality is that many customer service organizations have yet to balance customer satisfaction and cost efficiency. To remain competitive, organizations must figure out the most efficient way to keep customers longer, grow their share of wallet and make themselves more profitable.

Providing great customer service while keeping costs down can be particularly challenging in a call center setting, where a few seconds added to each call can translate into excessive costs. At many call centers, success is measured by keeping talk time down. I recall reading an article about how this approach went terribly wrong for one company, whose agents were literally hanging up on customers to take more calls. As a result, the company quickly lost a significant percentage of its customers.

> *There is a false assumption that a customer-driven approach to doing business is costly, but that's not the case.*

As these tighter economic times call for new ways to balance both customer satisfaction and efficiency, lean and mean companies are leveraging all they can to minimize costs without negatively impacting the customer experience. Can an organization have the best of both worlds? Great customer service and efficiency to boot? Today big retailers like Best Buy, Circuit City, Radio Shack and Wal-Mart are undertaking company-wide efforts to build efficiency into the customer experience by improving the coordination between their websites and their stores. A tighter multichannel service company can significantly reduce the number of incoming e-mails and phone calls from customers.

There is a false assumption that a customer-driven approach to doing business is costly, but that's not the case. Below, I've listed several practical solutions your organization can undertake to improve your bottom line without sacrificing the customer experience. When done properly, these solutions can also lead to increased customer satisfaction.

1. Improve first touch resolution (FTR). One of the most effective ways to balance satisfaction and cost is by solving customer issues during the first point of contact. Have you ever contacted a customer service department to get an issue resolved and felt like you were being rushed off the phone? Well, you probably were. Why? Because service managers are under pressure to deliver higher volumes, which don't necessarily drive customer satisfaction. The service reps are charged with fielding and completing customer calls as quickly as possible. When customers have to call back numerous times, and send e-mails back and forth, not only does it irritate your customers, it costs your company more time and money.

2. Let go of your power. The only way your organization can improve FTR is by empowering your front-line employees and/or call center reps to handle customer issues when they arise. The primary reason why empowerment is such a key component of FTR is because coming up with the right solution to make the customer happy has to be left to the people interacting with the customer. And that means empowering them to be able to make real decisions.

Just telling everyone, "You're all empowered," is more likely to create disorder than increase customer satisfaction.

I hear managers always say, "We empower our front-line employees." But empowerment, by itself, is not enough. Just telling everyone, "You're all empowered," is more likely to create disorder than increase customer satisfaction. Real empowerment does give employees permission to make decisions, but they also need to be taught what that means and given the proper tools to execute it effectively.

3. Optimize your website. When your customers can find what they're looking for on your website as opposed to calling you direct, contacting a customer service rep or sending an email, the savings can be substantial. Not only does it help improve your bottom line, but when your customers can get answers to their urgent questions faster, it can also increase customer satisfaction.

With the right website in place, you can quickly answer most of your customers' questions, thus eliminating the need for them to use more costly channels. While it's virtually impossible to answer every conceivable question online, more than 80 percent of all customer queries can be answered with the proper content developed over time by listening and learning what your customers need. Make sure that you get the most critical information up on your website right away and then fine-tune the content over time. Always keep your information fresh and up-to-date; and ensure that the information you provide online is consistent across all of your communication channels.

4. Invite your customers to play. Can your customers help you perform a task within your operation to help you save money? Is offering a self-service option a viable way for you to reduce cost? According to the Frances X. Frei article, in the interest of filling orders accurately and efficiently, Starbucks trained its customers to place their orders in the way that helped Starbucks operations. Online auction houses like eBay have pretty much eliminated labor expenses by persuading customers to serve themselves. Virtually all of the labor of buying and selling on the site is performed by customers, not eBay employees.

Think about your business and see if there are any areas of opportunity where your customers can play a part in the experience while lowering cost to you.

Lastly, remember to talk to your customers before introducing any new technologies or programs to reduce costs to your organization. You want to find out up front how the proposed changes will impact the customer experience. The last thing you want to do is eliminate or even water down a component of the experience your customers deemed valuable.

You know what's funny? When I think about the Gateway story and how we're introduced to some form of new technology on an almost daily basis, our need for hand-holding really hasn't changed that much. Even today we're still challenged with understanding all this high-tech stuff. Come on. How many remote controls do we *really* need to operate our home entertainment centers?

CHAPTER FRQs

1. Would you say that your company has mastered the balance of efficiency and customer satisfaction?
2. Are your line-level employees empowered to improve first touch resolution (FTR)?
3. Has your company taken the time to evaluate its website to determine how well the content addresses key customer concerns?
4. Have *you* spent time thinking about how you (or your department) can lower cost to the organization while enhancing customer satisfaction?

Chapter 15

A FISH ROTS FROM THE HEAD DOWN

The ancient Chinese proverb "a fish rots from the head down" means that any problem in an organization can be traced back to the organization's leader. How important is having the right leadership to an organization's success? Does Enron, Tyco or WorldCom ring a bell? Talk about examples! It is the leader's responsibility to create the right internal climate for an organization. While it takes a team to make things hum, it is ultimately the responsibility of the leader to set the tone and climate of the company.

My wife and I love to go to the movies. There's nothing like a good movie, a box of hot buttered popcorn, a cherry Coke and an *occasional* hot dog. We frequently visit two different movie theaters here in Minneapolis. Both of them are run by the same company, but the customer experiences between them are like night and day. At one theater, the ticket staff is always welcoming and friendly. The employees behind the concession stand are always smiling and ready to serve. To our surprise, some of the employees actually recognize us by name. Yep, we've seen a lot of movies. The employees there actually make us feel special, and have bent over backwards to make things right when (and if) they do go wrong. I met the theater manager once and this guy radiates customer service. He oozes it. He genuinely cares about how his customers feel and will do whatever it takes to earn their loyalty. A man after my own heart.

The employees at the other theater make us feel like we're an annoyance and are somehow generating extra work for them. One time we had a service issue with one of the employees, and we asked to speak to the manager. Big mistake on our part. This guy could not have cared less about making his customers happy. His customer service approach: if the movie is running, you should be excited. He was looking at everything else going on while we were trying to talk to him. His walkie-talkie was blasting away and we watched as he ripped into one of his employees. He was demanding, aggressive and had his employees intimidated and on the defensive.

Although these two theaters are not far from one another, they are miles apart in terms of customer service. It's very clear that the difference started with the leader.

A TALE OF TWO FISH

Home Depot grew to become the world's largest home-improvement chain largely on the strength of its skilled employees, many of whom were former plumbers, electricians and carpenters who were eager to share their expertise with customers taking on their own home projects. Home Depot was a loosely run organization. The people on the sales floor had a good deal of flexibility and autonomy. They took pride in helping customers find the right shade of latex paint, the ideal floor covering or that perfect shower head. Then something happened.

CEO Robert Nardelli joined the company in 2000 and worked to centralize operations and improve productivity and operational efficiency. According to a February 2007 *Wall Street Journal* article, service began to slip over the past six years. In order to cut costs the company started hiring more part-timers and added a salary cap that drove off the more seasoned workers. Among other things, the retailer also moved about 40 percent of its workers to overnight stocking positions. Before long, the company had employee morale issues. Instead of enthusiastically taking care of customers, workers spent most of their time huddling in the aisles complaining about management. In the meantime, customers had to fend for themselves, searching endlessly for someone in an orange apron to help them find the perfect drill.

In the Q4 2005 American Customer Satisfaction Index (ASCI) report, Home Depot had lost a lot of ground with an 8.2 percent drop to a score of 67. Home Depot's rival Lowe's, meanwhile, hit an all-time high score of 78. A University of Michigan professor and director of the National Quality Research Center attributed Home Depot's decline to a corporate culture that had shifted away from customer focus. Home Depot CMO Roger Adams said that "a focus on short-term stock prices and efficiency improvements over the past few years caused the chain to lose sight of customers."

Have you been to a Home Depot store lately? Enough said.

On January 2, 2007, Robert Nardelli resigned as CEO and now Home Depot is on frenetic quest to reignite sluggish sales under a new leader.

Yum Brands, Inc., chairman and chief executive David Novak is not your typical corporate leader. Mr. Novak views himself more as a coach and cheerleader than as the boss. He oversees one of the world's largest restaurant companies, which include notable brands like KFC, Pizza Hut, Taco Bell, Long John Silver's and A&W. Yum

Brands, Inc., has some 35,000 outlets in 112 countries and nearly a million employees.

In his recent book, *The Education of an Accidental CEO*, Mr. Novak notes that his worth as a CEO is doing "whatever it takes to get people fired up." He motivates his team members by giving them praise. He is always on the lookout to celebrate the achievements of others. He says, "The higher up the ladder you are, the more important it is to give credit rather than receive it." He often sends handwritten congratulatory notes to subordinates, signing them with a smiley face. The company is saturated in employee awards, including engraved silver pizza pans, rubber chickens, and $100 bills. Mr. Novak says, "Thank you" is "probably the most important thing a leader can say."

He's a stickler for excellence and sets the bar very high for his team. He maintains, "If you want to get noticed and promoted, it isn't enough to do just what is required. You must do more." He has also learned to listen to others' point of view, a hard lesson learned after his zealous attempt to market Crystal Pepsi while working in PepsiCo's beverage operations in the early 1990s. For those of you who remember, it flopped. *Time* magazine dubbed Crystal Pepsi one of the worst product ideas of the 20th century. That's all behind him, and now you might find him wearing a yellow foam rubber cheese head or giving out rubber chickens to employees. Mr. Novak describes himself as "the one among the Brooks Brothers suits with his shirttail sticking out."

Yum Brands' stock has quintupled since going public.

Moral of the story:
It doesn't matter if you're running movie theaters, home-improvement stores, or fast-food restaurants, at the end of the day it all comes back to leadership.

CALVIN'S LEADERSHIP TIPS

1. Never accept mediocrity. Allowing poor players to hang around too long is one of the fastest ways to bring an entire team and organization to subpar performance levels. One of the biggest challenges for the service industry is finding and retaining quality talent. To help offset this labor challenge, some hiring managers accept below-average employees to fill the slot or to have a "warm body" in a position. But what happens is that your A/B players soon realize they are making up for all the inadequacies of the poor players. This environment soon leads to morale issues, and in the worst case your A/B players begin to take on the behaviors of the others because it's acceptable. As Jim Collins says in his book, *Good to Great*, "get the wrong people off the bus."

2. Praise often and openly. An often and openly (O&O) approach is the pathway to creating passionate employees. Most often, many leaders forget that it's the small frequent acts of appreciation that mean the most to employees. Not showing someone how much you appreciate their contributions is like making them go away. Remember, assuming someone knows how much you appreciate them will never, ever motivate them to higher levels of performance. Let them know how valuable they are to the team and the organization.

Mistakes are just hiccups disguised as opportunities.

3. Learn and move on from mistakes. Listen, we're only human and we all make mistakes. No one is flawless. We can do things with the best intentions and sometimes they still may not produce the results we hoped for. Don't beat yourself up about it. Mistakes are just hiccups disguised as opportunities. If you make a mistake, the wrong way to deal with it is to not own up to it. If you've dropped the ball, or made a poor decision, take responsibility for it and don't let it happen again. But most important, don't swim in a pool of guilt, shame or embarrassment. Learn from it, live with it and move on from it.

4. Select for success. Always hire for attitude and passion. Cultivate an environment of candor where your team feels comfortable making suggestions to improve customer service delivery. Your best ideas will most likely come from the front lines. Reward your employees for their contributions and always celebrate successes –

even the small ones. Remember, your only real sustainable, competitive advantage is your people.

CHAPTER 15 FRQs

1. When *you* make a mistake, how much time do *you* spend wallowing in self-pity?
2. As a leader, do *you* cultivate a learning or a punishing environment?
3. When was the last time *you* said "thank you" to an employee for his or her contributions to the team?
4. How often do *you* apply the open and often (O&O) praise approach with employees?
5. How much time do *you* spend making sure that you hire the "right" candidate the first time?
6. How often do *you* celebrate team successes?

Final Thoughts

What are you going to do now that you've read this book? I know some people will continue to talk a good game, but do nothing. For some it will remain *business as usual*. Why? Because creating an FRCS culture requires work. Sadly, it's not until things take a drastic turn that everyone's attention is engaged. By then, the damage has already been done. Don't wait! Start making FRCS changes within your organization today.

While this book offers many ideas to rescue your customers from the world's customer service woes, don't become overwhelmed and try to implement everything all at once. That's where a lot of companies make their biggest mistake. One of my favorite adages is "inch by inch, everything's a cinch." Just focus on accomplishing three or four FRCS initiatives a year. Execute those to perfection, and then move to the next three to four and keep moving forward. Before you know it, you'll be rescuing more customers than you've ever imagined.

In the summer of 2007, I conducted an all-day customer service workshop for the Nashville Symphony team. Their patrons were frustrated because they were getting bombarded with phone calls from the Symphony. One group was making outbound calls about tickets. Another group was making outbound calls about donations. They also had another group designated to take inbound calls about tickets. In January 2008, they decided to rearrange their phone room to better meet the needs of their patrons. In an effort to improve efficiency and eliminate the possibility of patrons receiving multiple calls, they combined the three teams and now have Patron Service Specialists, each of whom has been assigned around 1,200 patrons who fit a certain level of giving and/or ticket subscription. Their patrons now only have to interact with one person to purchase tickets, give donations, handle rentals or catered events, or inform them about possible upgrades to a box.

"In any moment of decision the best thing you can do is the right thing, the next best thing is the wrong thing, and the worst thing you can do is nothing."
Theodore Roosevelt

According to the Symphony's president, Alan D. Valentine, "We've seen immediate dividends with higher donations from patrons and higher renewal rates because they feel they are getting a personal, high level of service from us. We still have a small group making outbound calls for new donors and ticket buyers, but they are a part of this overall group and are coordinating their efforts so we are working as a unit, not as three separate groups with three separate managers."

Yes, this is a simple solution to a major issue, and look at the payoff. According to Mr. Valentine, they are in fact the first symphony that they know of that has gone to this type of setup. He said, "Everyone else still has different groups making calls to the same customers about different things. We feel good about it."

What's the biggest difference between the Nashville Symphony and a lot of companies out there today? They actually did something to improve their customer service needs. No lip service, no empty promises, no well, maybes. They just took action. I want to encourage you to do the same. All you need are the three Ps – a **P**lan, **P**assion and **P**erseverance.

Don't just talk about customer service! *Be* about it!

BE FANATICALLY RELENTLESS!

Sources

American Customer Satisfaction Index (ASCI). Ann Arbor: University of Michigan, 2005, 2007.
Bauerlein, Valerie, and Robin Sidel. "Bank of America Uses Retail Tactics to Raid Manhattan." *Wall Street Journal,* October 21, 2006.
Conkey, Christopher. "Libraries Beckon, but Stacks of Books Aren't Part of Pitch." *Wall Street Journal,* October 21, 2006.
Customer Champions in European Companies Study, 2001.
De Lollis, Barbara. "As Hotels Upgrade, Items Left Behind." *USA Today,* October 3, 2006.
De Lollis, Barbara. "Ritz Loosens Up Its Tie to Change with the Times." *USA Today,* December 26, 2006.
Denove, Chris, and James D. Power IV. *Satisfaction: How Every Great Company Listens to the Voice of the Customer*. New York: Portfolio by Penguin Group, 2006.
Frei, Frances X. "Breaking the Trade-Off between Efficiency and Service." *Harvard Business Review*, November 2006.
Gibson, Richard. "Business Bookshelf: Pitchman in the Corner Office." *Wall Street Journal*, October 24, 2007.
Harari, Oren. *Break from the Pack: How to Compete in a Copycat Economy*. Upper Saddle River, NJ: 2007.
Horovitz, Bruce. "More Takeout Orderers Are All Thumbs." *USA TODAY*, January 4, 2008.
Kazanjian, Kirk. *Exceeding Customer Expectations: What Enterprise Rent-A-Car Can Teach You*

about Creating Lifetime Customers. New York: Currency by Doubleday, 2007.

Kranhold, Kathryn. "Client-Satisfaction Tool Takes Root." *Wall Street Journal*, July 10, 2006.

Lencioni, Patrick. *Silos, Politics & Turf Wars: A Leadership Fable about Destroying Barriers That Turn Colleagues into Competitors.* San Francisco: Jossey-Bass, 2006.

Michaels, Daniel. "No, the CEO Isn't Sir Richard Branson." *Wall Street Journal*, July 30, 2007.

MSN Money's Customer Service Hall of Shame, April 2007.

Poscente, Vince. *The Age of Speed: Learning to Thrive in a More-Faster-Now World.* Austin, TX: Bard Press, 2008.

Restaurants & Institutions 2008 New American Diner Study.

"Sprint Hangs Up on High-Maintenance Customers." *Reuters*, July 9, 2007.

Strativity Group, Inc. "Doing Business Right Now – Your Customers Won't Wait." White paper. 2007.

Don Thompson's quote courtesy of National Restaurant Association's *Smart Brief*

"2007 *1to1* Customer Champions." *1to1*, April 2007.

Welch, Jack, and Suzy Welch. *Winning: Everyone Wants to Win, Not Everyone Knows How.* New York: HarperCollins, 2005.

"What Does It Take to Win?" *1to1*, January–February 2007.

Zimmerman, Ann. "Home Depot Tries to Make Nice to Customers." *Wall Street Journal*, February 20, 2007.

About the Author

CALVIN STOVALL is President and CEO, speaker, leadership coach and customer service trainer for The Professional Advantage, Inc. based in Minneapolis, Minnesota. With more than 15 years in the hospitality industry, Calvin served as vice president of marketing with Hilton Hotels Corporation, where he was responsible for the brand marketing and public relations efforts for more than 150 Homewood Suites by Hilton Hotels. While under his leadership, Homewood Suites by Hilton was voted best in class by numerous consumer advocacy publications, including *Consumer Reports,* and recognized four times by J.D. Power and Associates for its unwavering commitment to product and customer service quality.

Today, Calvin utilizes his hospitality and management expertise to help his clients better understand and appreciate the importance of delivering exceptional customer service every day and how it can lead to competitive advantage. He also works closely with managers on leadership development and with teams to help them improve overall communication and effectiveness. His unwavering commitment to consistently deliver quality customer service to each and every client has contributed to the company's continued growth and success. His infectious personality and high-energy approach bring excitement to every project.

Calvin is a professional member of the National Speakers Association, Midwest Society of Association Executives and the American Society of Training and Development. He holds a B.S. in business management from Chicago State University and a master's degree from Cornell University's School of Hotel Administration. Mr. Stovall is a certified practitioner in administering and interpreting the PRO-360 Feedback Report, Myers-Briggs Type Indicator personality inventory and Herrmann Brain Dominance Instrument training tools.

Calvin, along with his lovely wife, Taisha, and vibrant son, Caden Daniel, resides in Minneapolis.